HERBERT BRENON:

AN AMERICAN CINEMA ODYSSEY

For Naomi
best wishes
Ian Graham

IAN GRAHAM

ISBN 9781521465936

For Ava and Charlotte

CONTENTS

Acknowledgements

This book evolved out of research I conducted at University College Dublin in the early 1990s, on the subject of the Irish born filmmaker, Herbert Brenon. I would like to acknowledge University College Dublin, and the library of the Irish Film Institute, where I did my original research at that time. In Britain, I spent a summer viewing many Herbert Brenon films at the National Archive, and acquainting myself with research material, at the British Film Institute, with much support from their staff. In the United States, the George Eastman House Museum in Rochester, New York was unfailingly supportive, and in this context, I would like to thank Nancy Kauffman for her expertise. I would also like to thank Kristine Krueger, of the Academy of Motion Picture Arts and Sciences, Margaret Herrick Library, in California. Film historian, Anthony Slide also shared some of his knowledge, particularly on the career of actress, Mary Brian who had appeared in a number of Brenon films. In my many trips to the United Kingdom, Photoplay Productions were very helpful to me. I would like to express my appreciation to the renowned film historian Kevin Brownlow, for sharing his knowledge with me, during our many discussions.

- **Ian Graham**

Beginnings

The Irish parents of the noted film director, Herbert Brenon, were writers, with interests in politics and theatre. Edward and Frances, were Church of Ireland by faith. The couple lived for a time in Paris. Frances enjoyed the theatrical and literary world. She took drama lessons at the studio of the celebrated French actress, Sarah Bernhardt, while her husband concentrated on his writing. They would sit together in cafes, around the River Seine, comparing English and French theatre. They were to imbue their children, with a love of the French language and culture. From her time abroad, Frances developed a reputation for running sophisticated literary salons. The Salon concept, originally an Italian idea of the seventeenth century, became even more synonymous with French literary circles, of the seventeenth and eighteenth century. People with a common interest in literature and philosophy would be brought together by a hostess, (for the Salons were usually run by women) and offered dynamic women, a central platform where issues would be discussed, among invited guests, at the home of the hostess. Frances excelled in this role, was much respected, for her well run salons and her extensive knowledge, of literature and the arts. In the 1870s, Edward became fascinated with the Italian nationalist movement and the successes of the Risorgimento. The couple decided to move to Rome. Edward began writing poetry, inspired in no small part, by the fervours of the recent achievements of Italian unification, and by his new found hero, Cavour. In Italy, Edward concentrated on his writing, mostly poetry, but it began to take a more political form, as he became wrapped up with recent history and contemporary, Italian politics and nationalism. He observed many parallels with Ireland. Edward, now had a somewhat ambitious vision for himself. He would return to Ireland, would enter Irish politics, but with the intention of taking a seat at the Westminster parliament, in London. He hoped to argue for Home Rule for Ireland. In 1874, they settled in comfortable Kingstown, on the south coast of Dublin. The couple were staunch nationalists, looking forward to a time when Ireland would have significant independence from the United Kingdom.

The family home, at 25 Crosthwaite Park, was positioned near the bustling harbour and the elegant, Royal Irish Yacht Club. It was a fitting location, for a couple, ambitious in the field of politics and art. A small private park was situated, in front of the row of spacious, terraced houses. The couple became friendly with the leader of the Irish Parliamentary Party, Charles Stewart Parnell – who, when not at the Westminster Parliament – would often attend dinners and functions, at their home in Kingstown, where Home Rule for Ireland, was naturally a topic of discussion. Edward was very briefly a member of the Irish Land League, an affiliated organisation, which did much fundraising in the United States, while Frances proved gifted and adept, at hosting cultural events, where personalities like Oscar Wilde and politicians would visit. Ireland was still under British control at the time, and Royal Visits by the British monarch, accompanied by British politicians, would sometimes arrive by ship, at Kingstown Harbour.

This was the type of milieu that Alexander Herbert Reginald St John Brenon, was about to enter. He arrived in Dublin, on January 13, 1880, to a family comprising of his sister Roma, and two elder brothers, Algernon and Chandos, who made much of the beautiful park outside their home for playing.

Edward's interests in Westminster politics and more outlets for his writing, soon became a persuasive argument, for a move to London. The English census shows the Brenon family; Edward, Frances and their four children, living in the district and parish of Fulham, London, in the county of Hammersmith. The family had two domestic servants, a cook and a maid. The outspoken Edward would later edit a couple of magazines, but was fired by the owner of one of these London publications, for his advocacy of Home Rule for Ireland. The earliest record of Herbert Brenon's English schooling is that he attended a Miss Bourne's, kindergarten school, before he entered the preparatory school, for St Pauls, at Colet Court London, in 1889. The governance of St. Paul's school was in the control, on Dean Colet's wishes, of the Mercers Guild, and remains so to this day. John Colet, had been the Dean of St Pauls Cathedral, friend of Erasmus, who he had met at Oxford, and had inherited a vast fortune from his father, and was committed to directing his money, towards educational progress. By the 19th century, the school had moved to Hammersmith, and the High Master, Frederick William Walker, ordered that a preparatory school, be developed, alongside the established grammar school. At Colet Court, Herbert was noted for his good conduct, and participation in school games. He stayed here, till December 1892, before moving on to Kings College

School, located in the Strand area of London. The area had a somewhat Bohemian quality, and was home to many writers and artists. The Strand area of London, stretching from Trafalgar Square to Temple Bar, at Fleet Street, contained theatres of every possible hue. At school, Brenon organised a dramatic society, when he was just fourteen years of age. He wrote plays and acted in them, mostly in the style of the popular, lurid, penny dreadful magazines of the day. At school, he was with many English boys who would go on to serve in politics and English public administration. In later years, when he was famous as a film director, with a justifiable reputation for excessive publicity, it was popularly thought he had been schooled at Eton.

Vaudeville Man

Relations between the ambitious, but sometimes incautious, Edward, and the sophisticated, Frances, had become fraught, which led to a permanent separation. Plans for a life in politics had not worked out. In 1896, the family left for America, a move helped by the fact that Brenon's elder brother Algernon, had recently married, and was anxious to start a new life in the United States, with his young bride. Initially, the family settled in Pennsylvania. Herbert was sixteen, and ambitious to join the workforce. He found work in a real estate office in Pittsburgh. This activity did not fire his imagination. He was looking for adventure and challenges, and he toyed with the idea of joining the American army, although nothing came of this. The Brenon family moved to New York, in 1896. That same year, Thomas Alva Edison, unveiled his Vitascope invention, at the Koster and Bial Music Hall, on Broadway. Several films were projected onto a large screen, including a hand tinted film, to a delighted audience. "When the hall was darkened last night a buzzing and roaring were heard... an unusually bright light fell upon the screen. Then came into view two precious blonde young persons of the variety stage, in pink and blue dresses, doing the umbrella dance with commendable celerity. Their motions were all clearly defined. When they vanished, a view of an angry surf breaking on a sandy beach near a stone pier amazed the spectators. The waves tumbled in furiously and the foam of the breakers flew high in the air... a skirt dance by a tall blonde completed the views, which were all wonderfully real and singularly exhilarating. For the spectator's imagination filled the atmosphere with electricity, as sparks crackled around the swiftly moving, lifelike figures. There were loud calls for Mr. Edison, but he made no response".

From the 1880s, until its slow demise around 1930, vaudeville was the most popular form of live entertainment in America, both in the cities, and in towns and villages, across the country. An evening of vaudeville, was essentially, a variety show, comprising multiple acts, of humour, music, acrobats, and perhaps some short extracts from serious drama, thrown in for good measure. In New York, Frances Brenon began teaching elocution, and Herbert found work in the office of a theatrical booking agent, named Joseph Vion. By night, Brenon worked as an usher, at the recently opened Weber and Fields music hall, where vaudeville was the main attraction; here Lew Fields and Joe Weber, were hugely popular among New Yorkers, with a series of routines, often dealing humorously, with the challenges of daily living for newly arrived immigrants, in the United States. One of the most popular showcases for vaudeville was, The Academy of Music. It had gone from a somewhat decadent interlude, in the 1870s, when masked balls on a French theme, were popular, before eventually turning to Vaudeville, to bring in the crowds. Brenon found work here, for the theatrical show, Sporting Life, uttering the line "program of the races" and gaining his first, small moment of fame. He was working for the noted theatre manager, Augustin Daly, during the 1898 season. Daly had an autocratic style, but his achievements were substantial. "Augustin Daly loved the theatre for its own sake", a contemporary critic would write.

"The enthusiasm of his youth never died. He was a man of taste and scholarship and courage. He believed in the drama as a fine art."

Brenon would later cite Daly and the Shakespearian actor Walker Whiteside, as people who taught him much about acting, and management. Brenon appeared in a number of small roles, including playing a Cadet, in a production of Cyrano de Bergerac, and with Whiteside, gained experience in a wide range of productions, including minor roles in Hamlet. In America, Brenon saw his life as a great adventure. He was an energetic Irish immigrant moving forward, realising his ambitions.The concentration on theatrical activities, where he could bring his European background and sensibility to play, was helpful. His family, for the most part, were with him in America. Indeed, Brenon wasn't so adventurous, that his mother didn't come with him everywhere. In that sense, a permanent aspect of late nineteenth century Dublin culture and life, with first-hand accounts of Parnell and Oscar Wilde, travelled with him to the United States. The struggles for Irish freedom and Home Rule were common themes in his life as his mother Frances kept the imagery of Ireland alive in his imagination. Frances Brenon would continue to be a major influence on her son throughout his theatre and film career, often visiting the sets and commenting on the actors.

The city of Minneapolis located on the west bank of the Mississippi river, was the location of a very vibrant theatrical stock company. It was run by Dick Ferris, and operated out of the Lyceum theatre. Publicity here was something of an art form, large balloons, took to the air as a means of advertising, and Dick Ferris was an extrovert character, who excelled at generating publicity for his productions. Ferris would run regular writing competitions, where the prize, was often seats at one of the Lyceum shows. It is likely, that some of Brenon's own showmanship, developed when he joined this theatre company. The popularity of stage shows, which focused on America's ever expanding frontier, was evidenced in *Way Out West*, a Cowboy and Indians drama, in which Brenon appeared, in October 1902. In those days, Minneapolis was a place where creativity was encouraged. Herbert's mother, Frances St. John Brenon, was now about to use her skills, in drama and voice coaching, to set up a School of Dramatic Art, in Minneapolis, which would be housed in the Lyceum theatre building. It would provide training to budding actors, and would have the benefit of a link to the stock company at the theatre, whose members including Herbert, would constitute part of the faculty of the drama school. Herbert was one of the speakers at the launch in April, 1903. America was certainly fulfilling, its reputation, of being the land of opportunity, even if, Herbert would refine his assessment of America more cogently, a decade later. While working in Minneapolis, he met a girl called Helen Oberg, (who performed under the stage name of Helen Downing). He liked working with her, and the friendship became more intense, in the weeks that followed. In 1903, in Minneapolis, Brenon staged a version of Shakespeare's comedy, *As You Like it*, a la fresco, in a forest on the shores of Lake Harriet. Brenon would play Touchstone in the play, and perhaps in life as well; the intelligent, witty, somewhat vain court jester, who provides a commentary, and insight, on the other characters in the play. Outwardly, Touchstone appears selfish, but proves capable of kindness as well, providing security to Celia, as he accompanies her, on her journey through the forest. It was Brenon's favourite role. Although, his talents were rewarded with promotion, the ambitious Irishman, was determined to be his own boss. But first, there was the matter of marriage. Helen was twenty one years of age, Herbert, twenty four. Instant soulmates with a common interest in acting and the arts, they married in New Orleans on the 18 February, 1904.

The couple planned to travel across America, as a Vaudeville act, under the name, Brenon, Downing and Company. For a few years husband and wife toured small towns and also larger venues, that were part of the Orpheum theatre circuit. It was a nomadic, transient type of life. A son Cyril, was born to the couple, in March 1906. They settled in Johnstown, Pennsylvania, a town which had developed rapidly , from its very humble Amish beginnings. The Pennsylvania railroad had been constructed, and the population was approximately 50,000, having grown substantially, from a decade before. It was in this setting from 1908-1909, that the couple were in effective control, of the local theatrical stock company, although they continued to tour the country. Frances St. John Brenon, had written a comedic play called, *The Intruders*, and they began performing in this production, including stints in Los Angeles and Washington. The play met with some success and positive critical response. "Herbert Brenon is the life of *The Intruders*, a farcical kind of sketch act " noted the *Los Angeles Herald*, while the *Seattle Star* observed that "Miss Downing is a dainty ingénue, with a Parisian wardrobe".

Brenon would never lose his enthusiasm for the thrill of a tour, the unique experience of travelling, with a close knit band of actors. It was evident too, that his interests extended beyond acting. Entertainment, the exuberance of the fairground, the circus, public amusements of all kinds, enthralled him. He began a different kind of adventure, running a roller-skating rink in Johnstown, for a short time, with the skating, supported by the screening of films. This activity is entirely in keeping with the notion of films at this time, that they were somehow part of a wider popular entertainment form, which included the fairground, circuses and fetes and markets of various types.

The Nickelodeons had started in 1905; exhibition spaces for the screening of films, dotted in the cities, and around the country, often little more than converted stores, with a few benches set up for the spectators, and a screen put up in one end of the room. Films were approximately ten minutes in duration, which was roughly the length of a 35mm reel of film. The fledgling film business such as it was, began to be focused squarely on the concept of a single reel of film, as the commodity. This would later have implications when some filmmakers had visions, of an industry which would centre on longer films. However, the rise of the early cinemas, or Nickelodeons, as they were popularly called, meant that the movies were destined to occupy, more than a supporting role to vaudeville presentations. Herbert decided to use his savings, to purchase a Nickelodeon, in Johnstown. The Early cinema of 1895-1908, was essentially a cinema of attractions, as historian Tom Gunning has noted.

Actuality films, not fiction films, dominated at this time. The films reflected daily life in all its various forms from boxing matches, a train arriving at a station, or a wave crashing onto a shore. Even in the United States, the origin of the films was as likely to be French, or Italian, than American, and they were about showing an event or the activities of daily life, frequently completed within the frame, and often comprising of a single shot, or scene. The cinema was still a novelty. Not infrequently, people would come to the Nickelodeon, out of a technical or scientific curiosity. Brenon became a modestly successful exhibitor, who recovered his investment, and sold out two years later, with a reasonable profit. He had become fascinated by the potential of film, and with encouragement from Helen, was now determined to enter the film business, on the production side.

In the formative years of the American film industry, most of the production activity was concentrated on the East Coast of the United States. Film production was focused around New York, and New Jersey. A short ferry journey, brought the filmmakers from Manhattan Island, to their studios, across the Hudson River, in Fort Lee. If the recording of events had dominated the cinema at the outset, filmmakers were moving the cinema into the realm of drama. People with experience of other fields, were beginning to show an interest in motion pictures, as a new medium of dramatic expression. The rise of the profession of screenwriting was a subject of much speculation.

A significant exodus of writers, from the theatre and newspapers, were attempting to embark on this new career, where for the few, substantial salaries were available. In America, studios advised writers to, "Make your story clean, wholesome, and happy- a dainty love story, a romantic adventure, a deed gloriously accomplished, a lesson well learned, an act of charity repaid – anything of a dramatic nature which is as honest as daylight. Good deeds are just as dramatic as wicked deeds".

Brenon must have appeared attractive to the New York of that time – a man who in 1909 was superficially American, with a fair amount of local colloquial phrases and mannerisms – yet professed to be Irish, while also having an attractive polish from his education, at two of the best "toff" schools in England. He would frequently quote from Shakespeare, Victor Hugo and Dickens. The studios were beginning to look for writers and frequently advertised for stories. Brenon had a good knowledge of drama, and managed to secure a job as a scenario editor with a New York film company, called IMP, which had recently been set up by Carl Laemmle. The studio counted the film director Thomas Ince, and budding actress, Mary Pickford, among their company, as well as an actor from county Meath, called Owen Moore. In 1911, Brenon would script several films, which featured Mary Pickford in starring roles, including *The Dream*, *For Her Brothers Sake*, and *The Aggressor*. The studio was located on West 56th street, in New York, and according to writer Gertrude Price, "looked like a second hand shop", not a factory of dreams. The studio made fifty "one reel" films a year. When they expanded to "two reel" films, they were still generating an output, of a film, every fortnight.

Notions of Irish nationalism were evident in Brenon's film scenario, *Shamus O 'Brien*. It was based on a poem by Sheridan Le Fanu, which conveys a narrative of a fiercely proud Irish revolutionary leader of 1798, fighting the British, for Irish independence. One critic noted that, "the poem by the gifted author, Le Fanu, is a favourite with Irishmen the world over, because it crystallises a desire that is deep in the hearts of countless millions, namely, Home rule for Ireland. On this theme there has been produced a magnificent two reel subject full of atmosphere". During this time, Brenon was earning 75 dollars a week. Unlike some at the studio, he managed to get through a prodigious amount of work.

All for Her (1912) was Brenon's directorial debut and starred the popular stage actor and manager, George Ober. It was a sentimental story which explored the relationship of a young girl, with two older musicians. An important early production was a version of Camille starring the established theatrical actress, Gertrude Shipman. Brenon's talents for creating mood and atmosphere, began to receive comment in the press. *The Fugitives* was the beginning of a series of collaborations with the actor William E. Shay. The picture was shot extensively on location in Sing Sing. More ambitious and striking a chord with city audiences was *Leah the Forsaken*. This film was set in Manhattan and concentrated on the relationship between a Jewish girl and her lover, who happens to be a gentile, and the destruction of their genuine relationship, because of pressure from family and friends. *Vengeance*, offered Brenon possibilities with special effects, destroying an entire train for the film. This interest in vehicles, locomotives of all types, technical gadgetry, and the latest developments in telephony that the United States was pioneering, was a distinctive feature of Herbert Brenon.

The Long Strike was an adaptation of fellow Dubliner, Dion Boucicault's play. The story centres on Jim Starkey, who is due to marry Jane Learoyd, whose father Noah works with Jim, in the factory of their employer, Richard Readley. An incident happens, when Readley makes advances towards Jane. In an attempt to free herself from further unwarranted attention, she arranges to meet the employer of her father and boyfriend, at a location, near her home. Her father discovers details of the appointment, and arrives at the scene, armed with a pistol. Noah sees his daughter, briefly in the arms of his employer, and believes his daughter has been dishonoured by Readley. He promptly shoots him, and the process begins, where Noah starts to lose his mind. However, Jim Starkey is blamed for the murder, and requires the testimony of his friend, the sailor John Reilly, to prove his innocence. Brenon's interest in acting was still unabated, and it came to the fore in this production. In an elegant manner, Brenon takes on the role of the sailor, John Reilly, inscribing himself as a visual presence in the film, and in doing so, provides the vital information necessary to prove to a court, the innocence of one of the central characters. This was long before such a nuanced film approach, became synonymous, with other well-known directors, like Alfred Hitchcock. The film was a powerful depiction as one critic noted, "Of the transition from the sound to the unsound, of the creeping on of insanity".

Despite its many industries, pockets of invention, and the bravura,
developing architecture which by 1913, included the impressive
Woolworth building, the New York of the 1910s, was by and large, dirty
and undeveloped in many ways. The stench of unregulated manure dumps,
filled the air, thousands of dead horses and cattle, still had to be removed
from its streets on an annual basis, to try to manage infectious diseases. It
was also a city with its fair share of prejudices. While Brenon's winning
Irish charm and English private education, gave him the confidence to mix
well within different echelons of New York society, this was not the case
for the majority in the film industry. In particular, many in the acting
profession, were frowned upon, in civic society, and frequently not
welcome at church services. Brenon was very supportive of the idea of a
private, social club for the film community, and he attended the early
meetings, when the idea was initially mooted. The Screen Club, met first in
New York on September 11, 1912 and Officers were elected at a meeting
on September 28. Herbert was voted onto the board of Governors. The
club located premises, at 163 West 45th street, on Broadway, and opened
for the first time, on the evening of November 9, 1912. The official colours
of the Screen Club, were green and gold. The club had a cafe, library, a
music room, a grill and meeting room. It eventually numbered several
hundred members, and was the most important group of American film
industry professionals at the time, prior to the formation of the American
Academy of Motion Picture Arts and Sciences, in California, in the 1920s.

The choice of venue for some of the Screen Club's annual events, was
consistent with the film industry's new aspirations. The Hotel Astor, which

had opened in 1904, located in Manhattan, was a popular lavish hotel, with its impressive New York lobby, opulent, rococo and neoclassical, opulent ballrooms, and it's beautiful, roof garden and bandstand. The hotel became an important fixture of the New York social scene, and with its early association with the Screen Club, synonymous, with the coming of age of the film industry, and with the impressive, and evolving, entertainment district, of the newly re-named area of Manhattan, called Times Square.

Brenon was starting to take a leading role as advocate for the movie business, even as he filmed armed conflict between the U.S. Secret service and various assailants, for *Secret Service Sam* (1913), with dramatic action scenes, filmed on several boats, in the area of the Narrows. The same year Brenon directed an Irish themed drama, *Kathleen Mavourneen*. Terence (William Shay) and Kathleen (Jane Fearnley) are young lovers who intend to marry. Complications arise when the local squire, Bernard Cavanaugh (William Welch) becomes infatuated with Kathleen who he sees on rent day, and makes a proposal to marry. The film was based on the popular song Kathleen Mavourneen, written in 1837, by Annie Crawford and Frederick Williams Nichols Crouch. This Brenon version also seems to have been based on the play St. Patrick's Eve, by William Travers. The song became popular across America, due to the astonishing success of the Irish soprano Catherine Hayes, who toured the United States, around 1851-1855. Hayes was the first Irish woman to sing at La Scala in Milan. Among her repertoire of songs, Kathleen Mavourneen was a particular favourite. Later the song was widely sung during the American civil war. When Brenon released his film, even the title itself, would have meant something to American audiences. *Kathleen Mavourneen* got a very positive review from *Moving Picture World* and there was more evidence of Brenon's skill, at blending the elements in an imaginative manner.

An interest in historical projects was on display with an ambitious drama of the French revolution, *Robespierre* (1913). The director had fifty actors in the cast, supported by another 150 extras. Key scenes included, the Convention hall, the Robespierre salon, the place de la revolution, where Robespierre is executed and the recreation of scenes, supposedly set, in Notre Dame. Authentic documents from the era of the French revolution, signed by Robespierre were used by Brenon in the film, adding to the impression of authenticity, and creating an unusual, timeline effect. Brenon's work was continuing to attract attention and plaudits. In 1913, in Oregon, the *Daily Capital Journal*, would write, "Herbert Brenon, who has staged some of the most wonderful productions ever shown on the motion picture screen, has added another to his list of triumphs, in *Robespierre*. Meanwhile, in Texas, the *El Paso Herald*, remarked that Brenon was now considered, "the greatest director of historical films in the world today".

London, Paris and Berlin

As the film industry advanced, it became important to be able to differentiate individual films from one another. It became clear than genre had an important role here. The development of a star system also helped. Finally some prior knowledge of the content of a film, through the mechanism of a sophisticated publicity strategy, but also by adapting well known plays and novels, (with their own independent history) was the final element which helped in this process. Brenon instinctively understood, that a film could not be divorced from its social or cultural context, and adapting well known literary works, like *Les Miserables*, helped to shorten the need for explanation, when you were trying to attract spectators, to the picture house. In a somewhat similar vein, was Brenon's film adaptation of, *Dr. Jekyll and Mr Hyde* (1913) which is one of the surviving, early Brenon films. King Baggot in the dual role is utterly convincing, and his transformation from the charming well respected doctor, to the grotesque fiend, wandering the streets at night, is superbly achieved. Brenon and the post-production department handled the film, in an effective and dramatic manner, using clever use of dissolves. The Robert Louis Stevenson classic, provided rich source material, and the Brenon movie was striking, displaying a flair for the dramatic, and some strong compositions. It marked a significant development, in the horror film genre. The concept of making films on foreign shores was unusual, at this time, for an American film company, but the forerunner of Universal, had just such an ambitious plan. Brenon was put in charge. Carl Laemmle's final words before they left, "Go to England and make the best pictures that have ever been made". The film team departed for England, aboard the White Star liner, the Olympic, on May 3, 1913. On arrival in London, Brenon set up shop for the film company, at a premises, on Charing Cross Road. He was the Producer and director of his films. As Kevin Brownlow has noted. "Important directors were their own producers, handling the financial as well as the creative aspects of their pictures. Few were troubled by front-office interference because the front-office knew little about production methods".

Brenon was excited about the challenges of this European film adventure, and spoke positively, about his impression of the film industry in England. George Blaisdell, writing for the *Moving Picture World*, noted that: "Mr. Brenon praises the English theatres and refers to the most courteous uniformed attendants, the magnificent projection and beautiful music". He collaborated with the pioneer aviator, Claude Graham White, for *Across the Atlantic* (1913), the first of his European films. In 1910, the aviator had already accomplished the inaugural flight between London and Manchester, in under twenty-four hours. Later that year, Graham flew his Farman bi-plane around Washington D.C., over the White House, where he proceeded to land on Executive Avenue, creating something of a sensation. Graham White, advised on aeronautical matters, and did some flying sequences for the movie. It was shot around London and Hendon Aerodrome. Well known English landmarks and locations featured in the movie, including, Westminster Abbey, Buckingham Palace, St. Paul's Cathedral, The Strand and Fleet Street. The narrative concerned Wilbur

Norton (King Baggot) who has invented a new aeroplane, of interest to the United States government, but is been hounded by a foreign spy, Oyama (Herbert Brenon) who wants to steal the plans. In the narrative of this film, it is possible to appreciate, the start of the evolution of recognisable film genres, in this case, the spy or caper film. The success or otherwise of these projects, was going to depend on a number of factors, and Brenon was to prove adept, at bringing various elements together, to add to the value of his movies. The traits of hard work, resilience and obstinacy, as well as creativity, were beginning to reveal themselves, but he combined these aspects, with a remarkable degree of good humour.

He would need these qualities to meet the challenges of *Ivanhoe* (1913), an epic narrative of adventure and intrigue, featuring warring factions and mysterious, Templar Knights. Filming took place in the town of Chepstow in Wales, located on the west bank of the River Wye, an environment steeped in history. King Baggot played Ivanhoe, and would become a major star of the early cinema. He was one of the first actors, to be credited on a film, so Laemmle and Brenon, began the process of putting in place the star system, synonymous with the American cinema. It was another good example, of the developing genres, of the new film industry. Leah Baird played Rebecca of York. Brenon took on the role of her father, the Jewish money lender, Isaac of York. Walter Thomas was Robin Hood (the film featured one of the earliest film representations of the character of Robin Hood) with the distinguished English stage actor, Arthur Scott Craven, playing King Richard. Brenon's wife Helen, played the part of Elgitha. The production team stayed at the Bell Hotel, which was owned by the Thomas family. The British media were enthralled by the project. The *Daily Express* gave considerable coverage. A journalist from the paper got a small part in the picture and described his experiences, working with Brenon. "He was awfully keen on detail, that American producer. He had me thrown off the battlements five times, before he was satisfied, and in my next great comedy scene, where I was pushed into the moat by a Jester, he did not seem to care how much film he used, as long as I learned to go in, with the proper kind of splash".

Chepstow castle, the oldest stone fortification in Britain, was an excellent setting for the action. Hundreds of locals took part in the filming, and Brenon planned the scenes with precision, as he co-ordinated the Knights Templars, and the Normans and Robin Hood's men, as they went into battle. As the forces prepared to attack the castle, Brenon would rouse their spirits with his megaphone. "Fight like blazes lads, and there's sandwiches and beer when you get inside". *Ivanhoe* was the type of film that Brenon excelled at this time – a visual display of action and spectacle – which enabled him to concentrate on visual storytelling. While Brenon's mise en scene is strong, characterisation is weak. The protagonists are not consistently inscribed in the film text, so actions or events in the film, are not clearly motivated.

Instead, we have a great spectacle of dramatic action sequences, of horsemen riding across the English countryside, or battles outside the castle, as Ivanhoe tries to rescue the Lady Rowena. Nevertheless, the variety of camera shots and angles is extensive. Brenon cutting to close ups from time to time. He uses some remarkable depth of field shots, placing characters in three planes, creating powerful compositions.

As Kristin Thompson has noted of this phase in American film production. "Staging in significant depth began at the period around 1910 when scenes still usually avoided analytical editing. But cut-ins added a sense of moving right into the space. The combination of multiple planes of action with multiple views from different distances was a powerful means of absorbing the viewer within the action". The British Film Institute's copy of *Ivanhoe*, shows the inherent talent for set pieces, for the grand spectacle, which Brenon would execute, with even more skill and proficiency, as his career progressed. In London, 109 prints of the film, were distributed to an enthusiastic cinema public. *Ivanhoe*, was released in America, on September 22, 1913. An immediate success, it was an early example of the validity and importance of the feature film, as a distinct narrative format.

On Brenon's journey to Paris, he enjoyed the sights to be found, in the cosmopolitan city. The new location appealed to Brenon, he spoke fluent

French, and he had a new vision of himself, after the epic *Ivanhoe*, as an important artist, with something to say. He enjoyed sitting in Parisian cafes with smart pastel coloured suit, and straw hat, or taking boat trips along the River Seine. The development and advancement of a new art form was what Herbert Brenon was attempting to achieve, and he received enthusiastic co-operation from the French authorities, during his time in Paris. For his film, *Absinthe* (1913), he also began to develop a social conscience. Brenon and King Baggot visited the Latin Quarter, to observe the effects of the drink on the locals, as well as to get a sense of the authentic atmosphere. Paris was home to a range of different types and groups, including the dreaded Apaches. The Apaches, were a violent criminal gang that roamed Parisian society and streets, particularly around the Latin Quarter and Montmartre in the late 19th and early 20th century. Liabeuf, a famous Parisian apache was guillotined by the French authorities, in July 1910. These historical elements had an important influence, on the making of *Absinthe* and the context of other Brenon films, which dealt with sordid Parisian themes. In *Absinthe*, Brenon pitted the individual against society, and also showed how a person, under the influence of such a substance, could go out of control, showing no respect for the law, or his own family. The film, not dissimilar to *Dr. Jekyll and Mr. Hyde,* presented a portrait of a man, experiencing a violent transformation in personality. During chase sequences in Paris, the city opened up and Brenon took advantage of the visual possibilities of the location. He captured the beautiful architecture of Paris with scenes along the River Seine, which provided some contrast, to the grimness of the subject matter. *Moving Picture World*, thought highly of the film, but considered, it would work, most effectively in France,"there the blind and reckless passions aroused by excessive indulgence in the drink will be better understood".

These European projects were testing Brenon, as he developed his creative craft of film director. The team departed Paris and moved on to Germany. In Berlin, Herbert stayed at the Hotel Bristol, a popular haunt of the time, on Berlin's leading boulevard, Unter Den Linden, located in the historic centre of the city. He had the company of Helen and son Cyril. They enjoyed Berlin's shops and cafes, and the Opera House. Brenon had an opportunity to explore the cinemas in Germany. He was most impressed with the quality of film presentation, with the timing of film programs (the Germans tended to screen films, which started later in the evening) and intrigued, at the higher amounts, that the Germans were able to charge in ticket prices – when contrasted with that paid by the poorer immigrant audiences, who came to see his films in America. In Germany, he made *Time Is Money*, with actress Leah Baird and also found a role for himself, in the picture. The film was full of action set pieces, including dramatic sequences, involving a Zeppelin, and motor boats. He made *Love or a Throne*, a romance film shot in Berlin, and filmed on a lush estate outside the capital. *Love and a Lottery Ticket* was a comedy, featuring William Shay and Leah Baird, as two struggling Americans, in Berlin. Filming complete, the Brenon's took the ship, from the German port of Bremen, and they were back in New York, by October 28, 1913. There had been much re-organisation and IMP had merged with several other companies, to become Universal.

Brenon now envisaged movies of similar duration, to that of a theatrical play or broadway show. This was his grand and optimistic vision for the cinema. However, Universal had a preference to make short films for spectators, who might have limited time on their side, or be in transit, simply waiting for the next train. The production and manufacture of a short film was easier, with less risk attached. In addition, many cinema owners were not well equipped for the lengthy musical accompaniment, required for feature film presentations. They saw the unique aspects of feature films, as problematic to their more makeshift business enterprises. They preferred one and two reel comedic films, and saw the feature film as a threat. In one sense, they were right. In a few short years most of the Nickelodeons were gone, to be replaced by larger purpose built cinemas.In essence, Brenon's vision for the American cinema required increased investment, not only on the part of film producers, but also on the part of cinema owners. So the issue of how long a film should be, was not trivial, but pertinent to debate, and a key issue to be resolved by the industry in due course. For the moment, Brenon would try to do the thinking for everyone else, and stick doggedly to his commitment to longer films. In December 1913, Brenon's cast and crew arrived in Bermuda, to commence filming the Universal production, *Neptune's Daughter*, starring the internationally acclaimed swimmer, Annette Kellerman. In previous years, Annette had experienced success at long distance swimming, out in the open seas, but had given it up to concentrate on more lucrative stage routines. This had led to a career playing in theatres, in Australia and Europe. By 1913, she was ambitious to be in pictures as well. "I am simply crazy about movies and I am going to appear in one", she told a journalist. *Neptune's Daughter* was a new terrain for the cinema, a fantasy world of mermaids and underwater filming, shot in a remote and exotic location, perfect for the fable like narrative. It gave Kellerman a very strong action role.

For much of his life, adapting *Gulliver's Travels* for the screen was a project under consideration by Brenon, but in later years, he would always cite expense, as a reason for not pursuing the venture. Still, *Neptune's Daughter*, was going to appease his appetite for fantasy and adventure. In Bermuda, when the small ship arrived, the locals gathered in expectancy. They waited to see if the swimmer would dive from the ship, or perform some amazing stunt. They were disappointed, when Annette Kellerman simply walked down the plank, and on to dry land. Although Brenon fell out with Captain Peacock, the screenwriter, in what sounds like the classic, perennial, Hollywood film dilemma, he seems to have been very supportive of Kellerman and interested in her ideas for the film. Brenon was extolling the virtues of filming outdoors, and producing work which he believed defined the cinema, with an emphasis on nature and landscape. The geography of Bermuda, presented many possibilities. The whole landscape was new, unspoilt and attractive. The production was shot on Bermuda's South Shore beaches, in the Crystal Caves and on Agan's island. In the movie, Annette plays a strong powerful heroine, albeit a mermaid, and the picture was full of action sequences, where the physicality of the Australian swimmer was used to good effect. It was visually very beautiful, with Annette engaged, in all manner of stunts in the water, including a swim with other 'mermaids ', in Bermuda's Crystal cave. The film was a fantasy and a love story all in one. In February 1914, the crew were enjoying the unique locale, and in good spirits.

A scene was to be shot which involved a scantily, clad Kellerman, engaging in an underwater tussle, with a villain, Roader the Wolf, played by Brenon. The water was approximately six feet in depth, and the tank contained thousands of gallons. During the shooting of the sequence, one of the glass sides broke. Kellerman received minor grazes, as she calmly and skilfully swam with the flow. Brenon panicked, and his left arm, according to one report was "laid bare to the bone". It took thirty minutes for Dr. Arton, to arrive. The injured were brought from the location, by motorboat, to the hospital, in Hamilton. From his bed in the Cottage hospital, Brenon managed to dictate a letter: "A friend is kind enough to write this letter for me. You know I pretty nearly passed...and am not out of danger... the glass took the initiative and broke, drawing the two of us through and turning us over. The rush of water carried us thirty feet from the tank. Miss Kellerman, I am glad to say, escaped with a minor wound on one foot. I was torn in six places by the jagged glass, how badly you may judge perhaps when I tell you that when the surgeons got me on the operating table they proceeded to take sixty-three stitches in me. I cannot eat or drink, and in my dreams sometimes I see an old pal... I am a little weary now. Please remember me to all my friends ".

The filming resumed, six weeks later, with the director arriving on set on crutches. The movie was released on 20 May 1914, in 7 reels, as a Universal special feature. The movie poster played on its unusual nature, including the surprising length of the film. "A weird, wild, wonderful spectacle in seven parts, staged by Herbert Brenon". The action orientated aspect of the film was found to be attractive. "Annette drowns a man who tries to drown her and then comes to the rescue of the King who is beset by swordsmen and wounded" reported the *Gotham Weekly Gazette*. "After they are all dead, the King recovers in time for a love scene taken against the sunset, which shows the rapid strides that photography is making nowadays". In addition, Brenon's use of nude sequences of his star, did not go unnoticed, by the critics. The *Variety* review wrote that: *"Neptune's Daughter* with Annette Kellerman should prove a large money maker for Universal, and have a wide circulation, for the fame of Kellerman as a water nymph ensures attention … while the exhibitor may quietly confide to his patrons they will see more of Annette in it, than they ever hoped or expected to" . The movie ran for six months at the Globe theatre, in New York. It made a million dollars at the box office, from an investment by Universal of 30,000 dollars.

The *Sydney Morning Herald*, was impressed with the film. The audiences in Australia, were said to be "ravished by the beauty and ingenuity of the film and the extraordinary, swimming feats of Miss Annette Kellerman, the world- famous swimmer and diver". It was screened in London, at the Shaftesbury Pavilion, to much acclaim, and Brenon's father, Edward St. John Brenon, by now estranged from Frances and living in London, was present at the screening. These early Brenon films exemplify the genre of spectacle, rather than that of story and character. Epic scenes and limited character development abound, and Brenon's visual style is given free rein. It may be argued that the Brenon / Kellerman films were exploitative, using the female form, as a site of spectacle, in part, creating a cinema that was built around the gaze, of a male orientated spectator. The counter argument, is that the signifying practices, inherent in the films of Herbert Brenon were more complex. After all, Brenon gave the Australian swimmer, action orientated parts, where she was the main star, influencing events through her actions. This made the narratives more progressive, than many of the films that Hollywood would make, in the decades that followed. Whatever, your viewpoint, it can be said, that Brenon was refreshingly open about the primal drives, associated with art and the cinema. "The primal passions and emotions that are the basis of poetry and painting cannot fail to attract the public, because they are deep-rooted in the human consciousness. The photodrama is simply the modern form of expression".

North and South

Brenon's contract with Universal was due to terminate on September 1, 1914, and he was eager to leave. He was disappointed that the success of the seven reel, *Neptune's Daughter*, had not swayed Universal about the feature film, as the future, for the American film industry. Even the advertising for Universal films emphasised Laemmle's approach, sometimes equating very short films with features. "Universal features are not padded. We are constantly cutting three-reelers down to two reels; and two-reelers down to one reel, in order to give you quick, sharp, snappy features, bristling with action". In 1914, Herbert was writing to other film producers, about possible collaborations, and letting key industry people, know of his availability. He sent a number of these telegrams, using the Universal studio address requesting, confidentiality from the recipients. Brenon's departure, was soon a fact, reported in the trade publications. On October 24, 1914, on its front page *Variety* wrote, "Universal has lost its star director, Herbert Brenon". *Moving Picture World* reported that he left his former colleagues at Universal, "with many regrets, but that he felt his greater opportunities lay in the way of feature production" . There was talk that he might join up with Adolph Zukor and Jesse Lasky at Famous Players Lasky (the forerunner of Paramount) but, he decided to go the independent route, in part, setting up the Tiffany film corporation.

Brenon was jovial, but serious at the same time, as he emphasised that much of his money was wrapped up in Tiffany, and that he would be keeping his "eye on the box office" even more than usual. Nevertheless, his view, in 1914, was that artistry was strongly reflected, in the box office receipts that ultimately accrued to a film.

He would turn to the American civil war for his next project. The threat to the disintegration of the perfect American political union, intrigued Brenon, as well as the substantial issue of slavery, that had been the focus of the war. He spent weeks researching and studying documents and photographs of the era. He had already made an attempt at a movie on this theme with, *The Dividing Line*, when he was working at Universal. However, *The Heart of Maryland*, an adaptation of a highly successful Broadway play from the pen of the acclaimed writer and theatrical producer, David Belasco, was an altogether more ambitious undertaking. Action and conflict was what the screen was about, and there could be no subject that provided more of this, than the American civil war. Still, Brenon would have to tread carefully, emotions were still high. He chose to make the movie on the west coast. Brenon's first production for Tiffany, was one of the earliest feature films made in California, evidence of Brenon's pioneering role, even at this stage.

The film director set about building an impressive church, which would contain the famous scene in *The Heart of Maryland*, where the lead character, swings from the clapper of the bell. The church which was seventy feet in height and elaborately designed, cost over 3,000 dollars to construct, a considerable sum in 1914, and was subsequently burnt to the ground, in the climactic sequence of the film. For this civil war film, Brenon had actress Caroline Dudley to play the lead. Caroline, who hailed from Lexington, Kentucky, was considered a beautiful southern belle in her youth. She married the wealthy lawyer Leslie Carter, and after becoming estranged from him, went on to have a highly successful career as a dramatic actress on Broadway. She became associated with plays like Madame Du Barry, and the stage version of *The Heart of Maryland*. She had an unconventional personal history, divorced from her husband, she now acted on stage to much acclaim, but to his horror, using her married name – Mrs Leslie Carter!

The movie featured many battle scenes, as Brenon put all his skill and energy, into his first independent production. Moving Picture World, captured the scene:

Commanding the cavalry is Captain Gunn, Major Light of the National Guard is in charge of the infantry, whereas the artillery is under Captain Ford. For a week preceding the battles these officers meet for conferences with Director Brenon and every detail of the campaign is discussed. Tests are made of seven kinds of powder, to learn which produces the most spectacular effect when exploded...On the day of the big scenes- a mild Sunday in the middle of December- twelve deputy sheriffs are on the side lines to control a crowd of 10,000 spectators, and in case of accidents, three ambulances with a corps of nurses are within call.

Brenon enjoyed the freedom of the wide open spaces. Even so, he had some doubts about the location. California lacked purpose built, indoor studio facilities. When the rains came, as sometimes is the case in California, it was dramatic, and impacted negatively on his attitude. Brenon was assisted by another enthusiastic writer and filmmaker. In a modest, makeshift studio, which he aptly named OZ, L. Frank Baum, was engaged in film production, in Santa Monica, making short films for children, based on his Scarecrow, Tinman, and Cowardly lion characters. Brenon hired some of Baum's facilities for his feature production.

The Heart of Maryland was the first feature length movie to be screened at New York's Hippodrome theatre, which had a capacity of five thousand. While some considered Mrs Carter, now aged fifty-three, simply too old for the part; they still watched her with some interest, furiously swinging from the bell in a scene, she had made famous on stage, as a more credible young lover, some twenty years previously. The critical response was mostly positive, James Shelley Hamilton remarking," it is one of the best civil war pictures that have been made", while the *Los Angeles Times,* in May 1915, was impressed with the ambitious "big conception" of the film, believing "the story makes startling picture". Even so, the flagship paper, in the city that would become the most nuanced about movies, remarked in its headline, perhaps helpfully, that some additional cutting would enhance the picture.

Brenon's career was already illustrating, the step by step evolution of the modern American cinema – not only through the various production outfits, that he interacted with, but also through the development of genre – the spy film, the adventure film, the melodrama and historical movies. *The Heart of Maryland*, was an important achievement, but Brenon nevertheless chose to cease activities at Tiffany, and instead moved back east, to the bright lights of New York. He was back in the city, where American art and commerce met. The film director would now develop an important creative collaboration, with a businessman, named William Fox. They were both cinema pioneers, key figures, at the forefront of the development of the American film industry, and a collaboration, was thus not unlikely. Fox owned movie theatres and wanted to move into film production and be surrounded by people who knew how to make films. In 1915, he formed the Fox Film Corporation in New York City, and Brenon was directing films for Fox that same year. In some respects they couldn't have been more different; Brenon with his dickie bow and sometimes pretentious artistic statements, which contrasted vividly with Fox's, " I seen it" or " I done it" utterances, when he wasn't mixing tenses, or declensions, as writer Upton Sinclair, so memorably recalled. Nevertheless, Fox was more engaged and enthusiastic, more personable than the cool and distant, Carl Laemmle. Fox liked to debate the merits or otherwise of individual films. More importantly, William Fox and Brenon were committed to the idea of feature films.

The New York city landscape, that Herbert Brenon was observing, appeared increasingly vital. He liked to move about the city, stopping at sights of interest. His passion for trains and architecture would see him visit Grand Central Station, which had recently completed construction. Often, he would walk down Broadway, stopping at Trinity Church. He would explore the richness of the episcopal, gothic revival church. He would look at the impressive bronze, east, south and north doors, which contained biblical inscriptions and referenced the history of New York. He would cross the road and saunter down the long narrow street, that is Wall Street, stopping awhile outside, observing the traders as they went in, and out of the Exchange building. When he had some free time, Herbert Brenon liked to go to boxing matches with his brothers Algernon and Chandos, and he was also a keen tennis player whose friends included several Wimbledon Champions.

At this time, the fan magazines were appearing. A fascination with the lives of the stars, was beginning to develop. "What is it like? What do they do after they leave the studio? Just what kind of home life do they enjoy?", *Photoplay* magazine, would ask for the benefit of their curious readers. Brenon's personal scrapbook, underscored the variety of his projects with Fox, showing his industrious nature, but also the Irishman's humour and sense of mischief. On the opening page, Herbert describes the contents. "Purely personal press pieces, picked promiscuously, pertaining principally, to pictures, pleasantries, paragraphs, perchance, peevish pecks". Among the films detailed in Brenon's scrapbook are, *The Soul of Broadway*, and a series of films with, arguably, the first, if unlikely, sex symbol, Theda Bara. The studio publicity, created a narrative, of a young temptress who grew up, amid the Pyramids. If that was not enough, she had purportedly a French mother and an Italian father, who had brought her up in Egypt, in their home, near the Sphinx! Her name was said to be an anagram for "Arab Death".

In 1915, when *Photoplay* magazine visited the set of Brenon's film *Sin*, a vivid account of Brenon at work unfolded.

"Herbert Brenon, the personality owning the face, is a slender, physically light young man of middle stature. His force is a spiritual force, but more than any director I have ever seen, does he live, embody and detailingly exemplify each character in the play, male or female, young or old. He burns himself up with everybody's passion. If the leading lady climaxes in a paroxysm of rage, grief or hysteria, Brenon is swept by half a dozen or eight emotional tornadoes as he shows her how".

The world of the Fox Film Corporation was speedy and brisk. Both William Fox and Herbert Brenon matched each other, not only in age, but in a brooding, aggressive, edginess. The *Evening Mail* noted that the first impressions of Brenon are, "rapid fire reactions and aggressiveness". Time is money was the motto and getting there first, the overriding priority. Girls looking for a break flooded the Fox offices, with no doubt, some tragic stories inevitable, when they failed to attract the right type of professional interest. However, for the most part Herbert Brenon was considered very professional in that regard. The filmmaker sometimes welcomed journalists to watch him for an hour or two, as he supervised the editing process. But the editing process was not what amazed, one visitor to his office, in 1915.

I started out of his office with Mr. Brenon and between the door of his private office and the elevator he was stopped just fifteen times by persistent folk who wanted 'A chance'. Most of them were girls. With all, Mr Brenon made it as pleasant as possible, but the answer was the same. 'You must see Mr. Mackay'. Two of the girls even got on the elevator to buttonhole the director, but he explained as gracefully as he could that he could not talk with them without an appointment and that they must see Mr Mackay to arrange the appointment. 'But', one of them insisted, 'I just want you to look at me'. But Herbert wouldn't break his rule.

It was becoming evident, and he had the experience of Germany to assist him in this view, that in order to raise the price of ticket admissions, more prestigious productions, which would attract middle class audiences, were necessary. He was also optimistic about the public's appreciation for the finer things in life. When questioned about the preponderance of pulp fiction in contemporary society, he seemed unconcerned. "Because the public reads a lot of trashy fiction, it does not follow that this trash holds a higher place in the public esteem than the works of Victor Hugo and Dickens". In *The Kreutzer Sonata* (1915) Brenon was attempting to move into more character-driven terrain. Leo Tolstoy's work had caused much controversy on its first publication. A serious meditation on the relations between men and women, it was written during a time in the novelist and philosopher's life, when he had embraced a more fundamentalist Christian outlook, with an emphasis on sexual abstinence. The choice of adapting the novel, shows the level of ambition that was integral to Brenon's personality. He had a sophisticated view of the cinema, and what might be achieved, given care, creativity, and professional presentation. In one scene, Brenon has the characters of Count Belusoff and Miriam Friedlander, seen visibly reading the Tolstoy novel, and the character of Celia Friedlander reproaching Miriam, for not following the example of her character, in the book. This creative, playfulness, this intertextuality and reflexiveness was a quality very much associated with the early development of cinema, when films were still sufficiently new for the mechanisms and mode of address, to be of interest to audiences. There was probably also an attempt to validate the film, as a serious work, by reminding the audience that a great novelist, provided the inspiration, for the cinematic representation that they were watching. There is definitely a transitional stage in which types of films, or genres of films are still not clearly delineated, or fully developed, and Brenon has some latitude in presentation and content, due to the fact, that the spectator, is still interested in the novelty of the new medium. These factors increased the freedom of Brenon, to express his ideas in an original way and still gain audience acceptance.

The Soul of Broadway (1915) was another venture into the world of complex, almost noir like, underhand female protagonists. Brenon's female characters are usually powerful, but sometimes are let down by the law, or by the amorous nature of their sexuality. Here, he had another vamp like actress in Valeska Suratt, once described as the most daring woman in Vaudeville. "Suratt is immediately, as far as the public is concerned, associated with high life, the Broadway life, the kind of life the public reads of and doesn't believe, but would like to try", wrote the nuanced trade paper, *Variety*. "It tells a brazen tale, brazenly, Suratt, as the central figure just fits". In June 1915, Brenon was on location in Atlantic City, New Jersey, for the film, shooting scenes on the beach and on its famous boardwalk, and using the attractive interiors of the Hotel Alamac, for key scenes in the film, as well as headquarters for the production, during the shoot. Guests at the hotel were said to be "spellbound" as they watched Brenon and his team take over the hotel, to shoot scenes of actor George Middleton, making advances towards Valeska Suratt, in some adjoining rooms. Huge arc lights, flooded the hotel with illumination, and Suratt was said to be "lavishly attired in a décolleté gown of dark blue spangles". Brenon was in vibrant form as he directed the film.

"Try to kiss Miss Suratt, draw closer. Compress your lips. Nearer, nearer", Brenon instructed his cast. *The Soul of Broadway*, was as much about fashion as narrative, even the advertising for the film, played up the amount of costume changes, which Suratt would undergo in the film. During the filming, Brenon treated himself by purchasing a brightly coloured, six cylinder, Japanese, touring car, with the initials HB engraved on the vehicle.

A Daughter of the Gods

Despite his penchant for literary adaptations, Brenon had always vowed to return to the world of fantasy, an area in which he believed, the cinema excelled. He wanted to collaborate further with Annette Kellerman, but this time, on an even more ambitious scale. William Fox looked perfect, as the moneyed fall guy to make it happen! Before travelling to Jamaica, to shoot *A Daughter of the Gods*, Brenon visited some galleries, including New York's, Metropolitan museum. He spent time studying the work of artists including Jose Villegas, Alexander Cabanet, Sorolla Y Bastida, John H. Twachtman, Winslow Homer and Rodin. He was especially interested in examining land and sea effects, and of course composition, and poses of the human body. "What is the motion picture at its best, but painting and sculpture brought to life", he emphasised. He wanted to produce a work of art, as well as a piece of entertainment. Not everyone, though, was thrilled about the prospect of a new Kellerman film. The *Los Angeles Times* in 1915, reported that a group of Ontario women, led by the local president of the Christian Temperance movement, were on a mission to prevent Annette Kellerman films from being made, or screened. The irony of the American cinema is the extent to which freedoms which were taken for granted in the early days of the cinema, would eventually be completely eroded by the end of the 1920s. Helpfully, at this time the censorship was limited and varied from state to state. It proved something of a bonus that Annette was a certain type of girl, who did not really have a life outside of swimming that could be commented on, or frowned upon. Basically, her father chaperoned her everywhere to swimming competitions and when he was no longer able to do that, he introduced her to a man, who she subsequently married, who continued more or less the role of her father, becoming her manager. There was something extraordinarily wholesome about Kellerman, and in her advice to girls not to smoke or drink cocktails, she won approval from their parents. The appeal of Annette stretched into the Ivy League as well. Dr. Dudley A. Sargent, a Harvard University academic, announced that Annette was "the perfect woman", because she most closely resembled the Venus de Milo! *A Daughter of the Gods* required many mermaids. Two hundred American girls were interviewed, for these roles, some recruited from lifesaving stations throughout the country. Annette did the swimming auditions in New York, to ensure their aptitude in the water, while no doubt, Brenon kept a watchful eye, as the final selection of girls were made. The general manager of the production was long time Fox executive, Winfield R. Sheehan. The movie featured large sets and at the other extreme, an elaborate gnome kingdom. Brenon was on an impressive weekly salary of 750 dollars. Minola De Pass, was recruited as his secretary, and would be an important part of Brenon's team for several years. Much of the filming was shot in St. Anne's Bay. Sharks were a constant danger, even in this beautiful sheltered cove. As filming progressed, the sharks darted across the bay, to meet up with Brenon's frightened mermaids. The filmmakers had a motor boat patrol, at the mouth of the bay, to ward off the sharks. The movie was a major news story during its production and the *Evening Ledger*, tried to help out, with an explanation of the approach taken by Brenon, for the filming of major scenes. "Every time a big scene was made on land or sea, six cameras were grinding away at it, from different angles. Two cameras were side by side at the point where the action promised to be most vivid and dramatic, and the other four were placed where they would get the action from new angles. Often the sixth camera placed at the most remote spot would pick up the action on the film in a way that made it superior to the work of all the other instruments, and this strip of film would be selected as the best for what the director wished to show". Brenon did his best to keep things moving, but he was at the mercy of the elements, and cultural differences in Jamaica, and not aided by the scale of his own ambitions. Still, he enjoyed the life of a would be colonial ruler during the time he spent in Jamaica and certainly dressed the part. The film went over budget, and not even the enthusiastic William Fox could forgive Brenon this time. It was stated that the movie cost a million dollars, and that figure was used extensively in the publicity, hence the reference to Kellerman, as the million dollar mermaid. However, press statements about budgets in the early days of the film industry were notoriously erroneous. If Brenon had spent nine months working on the film in the United States, rather than in Jamaica, and created such scenes of spectacle, it might have come close to a million dollars. In any event, it looked like it cost a million dollars, and that was the most important aspect. The American film industry was growing in sophistication, and there was a nuanced sense of how to generate maximum publicity, exemplified in *A Daughter of the Gods*. Here one finds in essence, the embryonic development of the modern

Hollywood blockbuster. This was an event film, with a highly focused director. Brenon foretold a new type of film production – the exotic, epic film, demanding great technical and artistic skill, with a personal signature from its director. Brenon was upbeat. "Naturally, I think *A Daughter of the Gods* is going to be the film sensation of the season; that is no more than can be expected of me, for I have been wrapped up in the production of it for more than a year. I will state this however, that the feature will not have competition of a direct nature for many years to come". After the shoot, the press continued to be intrigued, as to the extent of a rumoured falling out, with William Fox, but accepted, that they might have overplayed the quarrel as one journalist noted. "With the arrival of Mr. Brenon in New York all of the weird reports concerning him while away, vanished into thin air. The report that Mr. Brenon and Mr. Fox were at the parting of the ways was the first of the libels to be pinned down, for when the steamer docked, William Fox himself was at the wharf and greeted his long absent star director with open arms" .

If action and visual scenes of great beauty were the hallmarks of the film, Brenon also emphasised sex as part of the attraction of this film. Annette fully naked, in the scene where she prepares to dive from a cliff, into the ocean. In fact, *A Daughter of the Gods* contained the first scene of full nudity, in a mainstream film, by a leading star. Critics made much of this, and the reality that elsewhere, in many scenes, she did not bother much in the way of clothing, as she went about performing a variety of diving stunts. She would dive without any clothes, from a high tower into a dramatic sea of high waves, and then be pursued for what appeared to be a distance of some miles, by a dozen Jamaican natives. Similarly, Brenon was content to shoot scenes in a Harem, with young women sitting, swimming and dancing, with very little, in the way of clothing. When the press suggested, that the censors might object to some of the scenes in his film, he dismissed such concerns. "The censors won't object to my picture because they won't find anything to object to. You naturally wouldn't expect a bunch of mermaids to swim around in the water or dance on the sand in bathing suits. I never worry about the censors, because I haven't anything to fear from them". *A Daughter of the Gods* was released by the Fox film corporation, on 17 October 1916. The review in *Variety* was positive. "There are huge battle scenes, beautiful mermaids, wonderfully effective waterfalls, gnomes, nymphs, and so on until you are fairly spellbound with the enormity of the undertaking". The film magazines of the time were taken with the pictorial quality of the film.

In close to shore the shadows are falling, and the light space on the water is gradually narrowing down to the outer horizon. One long ray of light, however, remains behind and almost touches the shore- a ray of light miles long... Suddenly you see this remaining light ray begin to recede to the distant edge of the world. Just at this moment Annette Kellerman, pursued, leaps from a promontory and drops directly at the tip of the remaining sun ray.

A flair for fantasy was now going to be central to an understanding of Brenon, and it augured well for the future, indicative of what new cinematic worlds, the filmmaker might be able to create. In 1916, D.W. Griffith and Herbert Brenon were mentioned in a *New York Times* article, as film directors, who were paid more than the American President. On December 18, 1916, President Woodrow Wilson and the First Lady took a special journey to the Belasco theatre, for the Washington premiere, of *A Daughter of the Gods* – to celebrate their recent wedding anniversary, and the status of the American film industry – as one of the new big businesses of the United States. It was the first time that a United States President had viewed a film in a theatre, while in office. The production was "wonderful", according to the President. The cinema had come of age.

Nonetheless, the challenges of *A Daughter of the Gods* had strained relations between director and producer. Brenon claimed that his contract with Fox ensured his name would appear in all publicity connected with the movie. When this did not occur, he took exception and had his legal team, discuss the "oversight" with the studio. The dispute was resolved , but just as he had earlier left Universal, because he doubted Laemmle's commitment to the concept of the feature film, now he was ready to leave Fox, when the advertising for a feature film, did not give him sufficient credit, commensurate with his ego. The turbulent Irishman, had his own ambitious plans, and with investment from Lewis J. Selznick, (who had made a successful reputation as a film distributor) formed the Herbert Brenon Film Corporation. The business was said to have a million dollars in capital.

The new film endeavour needed a base, or permanent headquarters, to plan the projects and shoot interiors. The construction of the Ideal Studios and laboratories was completed in August 1916, headquartered on the Palisades, Hudson Heights, New Jersey, and leased for five years, to the Herbert Brenon Film Corporation. The studios had several stages and the total complex comprised of two buildings. Selznick was going to manage distribution and contracts. Also, involved in the new corporation was Stanley V. Mastbaum, an important Philadelphia cinema exhibitor, who owned fifty theatres at the time. Chandos Brenon, (who had an earlier career, in the Canadian Naval service), was now working with his brother, helping to manage the administrative aspects of the operation. George Edwardes Hall was in charge of the scenario department. J. Roy Hunt took charge of the photographic department and George Rush was the studio manager. Brenon was delighted with the quality of the new studios and announced that "no perfect work of art can be created without perfect tools. Imagine Paderewski playing on a cheap piano, or Kubelik on a $ 5 fiddle".

In this phase of independent production, in New Jersey, Brenon felt free to experiment more. He was also making decisions which he argued worked best commercially. One was the notion of concentrating on melodrama, as a narrative style, best suited to motion pictures. Brenon also believed that concentrating on women stars would be more profitable. Women made up a large proportion of the spectators at the cinema, and were fans of the visual and social narratives surrounding the leading actresses. It was also thought at this point, that the majority of men would prefer to see a woman on the screen. Later, film theory would argue persuasively that the relationship between the spectator and the cinema screen, was more complicated than that, for both sexes.

In August 1916, Brenon commenced production on *War Brides*. The pacifist film, based on a play by Marion Craig Wentworth was promoted with the tagline, "Womans struggle, throughout the ages". It marked the screen debut of Russian actress, Alla Nazimova. In *War Brides*, the character of Joan lives in a country, constantly at war. She loses her husband and a number of other relations in the fighting. The King of this strange country, issues a decree, that all women must bear children, for future wars. Joan leads an opposition against the King, "No more children for war", she protests, before finally killing herself. Brenon, expanded the one act play and made the film, not simply the story of a woman who opposed a King, and Empire, in respect of motherhood, but also, a vivid picture, of the effects of war, on all the people left behind, not engaged at the conventional battlefront, but with their own emotional and economic struggles to face, in the domestic sphere.

The film was made in thirty days, at the Hudson Heights studios. Nazimova, schooled in the techniques of Stanislavski, brought a beautiful intellectual rigour to her work. On the set, to apply his makeup, personally to the star was Max Factor, whose fame had initially come from his work in the movie industry, collaborating with filmmakers, like Herbert Brenon. The filming went smoothly until, Brenon desired Alla Nazimova to lose her beautiful demure looks and her passivity, and become an angry firebrand. She attempted the scene many times but her acting and the imaginative makeup, failed in Max Factor's words, "to satisfy the picture's famous director, Herbert Brenon". The solution, Max recalled, was for the director to have some musicians play a musical selection which she detested, and to play it badly. The actress lost her composure and Brenon got what he wanted.

Also visiting the set was Lewis Selznick, in charge of the business aspects of the production. He paid Nazimova a thousand dollars a day and would be photographed with her, handing over the money, generating further publicity for the film. The combination of Selznick and Brenon seemed to make the publicity, more hyperbolic than usual. *War Brides* was "directed by the master-mind, Herbert Brenon", according to one advertisement, while the *Yale University Daily News*, carried a poster for the film which stated that it was made by "Herbert Brenon, the directing genius". The film premiered to an audience that included William Randolph Hearst, Jesse Lasky, Adolph Zukor, and Schubert. There was more crossfire from William Fox, this time regarding *War Brides*. Fox attempted to come out with a similarly titled film, *The War Bride's Secret*, and Brenon took legal action to block this move.

In October 1916, Carl Laemmle, Lewis Selznick and Herbert Brenon announced that they had jointly leased the Broadway theatre in New York, and would be using the theatre to showcase works made by their respective companies.To an outside observer, Brenon must have appeared to have been inhabiting a most unusual, parallel world. As the European conflict intensified he was either on a beach in Jamaica, or in California, making an American civil war film. In 1916, he was in the throes of an anti-war pacifist film called *War Brides*, set in a fictional country, but probably somewhere in Europe. Certainly, he was proving his independent traits. The *Monroe City Democrat*, announced that, "*War Brides* is a masterpiece from the studio of Herbert Brenon, who is now recognised as the most progressive of all directors of photodramas". In total, the producers made about $300,000 in profits, from *War Brides*.

One of Herbert Brenon's ambitions was to increase the social status of the cinema. In his endeavours to do so, he often faced hostility. He became embroiled in a newspaper quarrel with Arthur Hopkins, a theatrical producer. Hopkins had commented that, "as a chance patron of the movies, I had almost invariably carried away one impression, bad taste". Brenon was incensed. In point of fact, the early pioneers were touchy, about perceived slights to their work, or to the purpose of filmmaking. Tenaciously, they had generated a film industry out of the ether, and no one was going to speak negatively about the cinema, or their vision for it. When Hopkins complained that many movies were promoted on the basis of cost rather than quality, Brenon retorted, "I will admit the heralding of spectacles on a basis of cost; that is a trick we were weak enough to borrow from the theatre". The film pioneers could be excessively secretive. They were generating tablets of stone, in some respects. The challenge of making films work commercially, was tougher than most people presumed. Film depended on certain skills and creativity and the practitioners tended to keep to themselves, feigning for the most, and for the publicists, a high living party style life. In addition, their industrial partners, manufacturers of film stock, cameras and other technology, also tended to stay close to them, resulting in only a somewhat less closed shop, than perhaps, magicians. They had the technological advances and new information first, and had tended to move on by the time these advances were more openly shared, with the rest of the world.

At this point, Brenon's work can be described as broadly in the realm of melodrama. He was keen to exploit the advantages of cinema over the theatre. "I am afraid, because the theatre has found it impossible to handle big action with anything like realism, that we have come to look down upon what we term melodrama. Yet we have only to open a newspaper to realise that life is melodrama. What is the Great War but the most tremendous melodrama ever enacted in the world's history. Five years ago, the war, if forecast on the stage or screen, would have been pronounced preposterous melodrama".

In the late winter of 1916, he was shooting scenes in St. Augustine, Florida. *The Eternal Sin*, was another ambitious undertaking, the Borgia story on film, starring Florence Reed, as Lucretia Borgia, and Richard Barthelmess as her son, Gennaro, based on the play by Victor Hugo. If the challenges of the film corporation in Hudson Heights had not been enough, he had got distracted by extraneous activities, investing in theatrical shows and appearing in them, at the same time. *Photoplay* magazine wrote, that "Not content with the misfortunes than can follow a picture director when they are going strong, Brenon decided to add unto them, those of a vaudeville producer. Nothing short of a dance pantomime in seven or eight scenes, with original music and a high- priced star, would suit him. When the final scenes of *The Eternal Sin* were awaiting his attention at Hudson Heights, Herbert was appearing personally in the out-of-town try-outs of his act, playing the role of Harlequin, because he could get no mime whose work satisfied him". Brenon became seriously ill, almost dying of typhoid pneumonia. He returned in January 1917, against the advice of his doctors, to direct the final scenes of the Borgia production, from a wheelchair. When the production wrapped, he was in a poor state, and went to Atlantic City, to fully recover. Despite the medical challenges, which impacted on the production of the movie, he got some positive notices for *The Eternal Sin*. "The growing reputation of Herbert Brenon as one of the big minds of picture-craft rests on something besides dollars and publicity, wrote the *New York Tribune*. "Whatever he does, he does with keen and penetrating knowledge of his implements, of the art possibilities of the profession, of detail and sweep of photoplay settings and exterior shots".

In March 1917, Brenon was in New Orleans filming *The Lone Wolf*. Brenon and Selznick had success with this action packed movie, which featured Hazel Dawn and Bert Lytell. It was based on the novel by Louis Joseph Vance. Brenon directed some dramatic sequences featuring a biplane, which was piloted by William Karl Hackett, who agreed to do some stunts for the movie. On one dramatic occasion Hackett lost control of the plane at 3,000 feet, when it got caught in an air current. The plane inverted, but Hackett managed to regain control, eventually bringing the plane down safely. "It was a bit too thrilling to be comfortable. The joke of it was the director thought I had turned the machine over purposely and complimented me, so I let the deception pass", he told the press. A film about the adventures of a lone wolf in Paris who befriends a female criminal, who turns out to be a secret service agent. Reviewers of the time were amazed by the effects in the film, and at how they had been achieved. "For speed and fascination this film has few equals", reported the *Quincy Daily Journal*.

The Fall of the Romanoffs

The scale and diversity of Brenon's ambitions and achievements was almost unrivalled, for a filmmaker of his time, and life, if anything, was about to get more complicated. Russia was permanently in the news. The Bolshevik revolution and subsequent collapse of the Russian monarchy in 1917, was clearly going to interest audiences. Brenon considered himself ideal for the task of recreating the tumultuous recent history of Russia on screen. *The Fall of the Romanoffs* (1917) was filmed at his studios in New Jersey. Brenon found a consultant for his film, in the guise, of an intriguing cleric, Sergius Trufanoff, better known as the monk, Iliodor. The monk had a fascinating background; a chaplain to the Russian Imperial court, Iliodor had previously studied at the St. Petersburg seminary. He had first met Rasputin, when the latter had come to visit the seminary. Iliodor became famous in the area, for his inflammatory speeches and attracted large crowds of fanatical supporters.

The monk introduced Rasputin to many people in Russian society. Later, Iliodor became concerned about Rasputin's undue influence, on the Imperial family and hence potentially, the political direction of Russia. As their friendship ended, Iliodor already under suspicion by the authorities for his political activities, was accused by Rasputin of stealing items of property, and of attempting to kill him. On the run from Russian agents, Iliodor made his escape, and set sail for New York. On arrival in the

United States, in June 1916, the monk began to have his story published in a New York Jewish publication. Later the serialisation of the story was suppressed. Iliodor claimed this was due to pressure, from among others, the Russian ambassador in Washington. In fact, so many aspects to the story and this production were unusual. The film was, ostensibly, not a project of the new Herbert Brenon Company, at all. Rather, the corporation and Lewis Selznick loaned Brenon the film director, to an entity intriguingly named, the Iliodor Film Corporation, headed by an Alexander Beyfuss. Nonetheless, the film was made at the Hudson Heights studios, and all Brenon's regular collaborators were involved in the production. What is undeniable, is that Iliodor provided a unique insight into the Russia of that era, and the personalities at play, attracting political, as well as popular interest in Brenon's film. For despite the misgivings of some commentators, Iliodor, had indeed, been in the company of these Russian figures.

In, *The Fall of the Romanoffs*, Rasputin (Edward Connelly) travels around Russia preaching and using his abilities to predict the future. A gypsy girl called Anna falls for him. Visually, Brenon's film displayed a certain grandeur. The film moved from a Siberian village, with its architecture of low squat houses and village vodka shop, where Brenon juxtaposed the image of a peasant cobbler, with the opulence of the inhabitants of the Winter Palace. In the film, Rasputin predicts the birth of a son, to the Royal family, and makes other predictions and is rewarded for his gifts, becoming a key figure in the Palace. When Iliodor (played by himself) sees the methods that Rasputin uses, he turns against him and supports the revolutionary forces led by Alexander Kerensky (played by W. Francis Chapin). The front of the Winter Palace was constructed, in Brenon's studio and *The Fall of the Romanoffs* also featured a perfect replica, of the imperial railway train.

It was an example of how a film could, by virtue of its subject, transcend the usual coverage in the review and gossip columns, and move out, to become prominent in the news and editorial sections of a newspaper. The public would now have an opportunity, via the cinema, to see a serious film presentation of some contemporary Russian history, which they had just been reading about, in the newspapers. The film was initially shown to around six hundred guests, in the ballroom of New York's Ritz Carlton hotel, on 6 September 1917. But there was drama here as well. William Brady, Head of the World Film Corporation attended, and announced that he had "beaten Brenon to it", in reference to Brady's own rival film, *Rasputin, the Black Monk*. After the screening, there was an altercation between the two men in the lobby of the hotel, where a number of blows were struck. Adolph Zukor, (later President of Paramount Pictures) had to intervene and struggled, to separate the two men. The film received its New York premiere on 23rd September, 1917, but negotiations were ongoing with the distributors, First National, and Brenon's film only became widely screened, after January 1918. Some changes were made to the film, by the time of its nationwide release, only increasing the unusual nature of the production. These included topical scenes of the appearance of Charles Edward Russell, a writer on economic theory, appearing before the Russian parliament. The film received very favourable comment, on its release. Mae Tinee, in the *Chicago Tribune*, noted that with Iliodor to advise, Brenon had produced a classic film.

During this time he was casting his son Cyril and niece Juliet, in small roles in his films. His wife Helen continued to be an influence on some of his story choices. *Picture Play* magazine described Brenon during the production of the film *Empty Pockets*. "Herbert Brenon sat before a sordid tenement room constructed in one corner of his Hudson Heights, New Jersey, studios. A sliding door at the side of the studio revealed a sweep of New Jersey countryside, vivid with the browns and reds of the autumn, in strange contrast with the wretched East Side room". By 1917, the United States was heavily involved in the First World War, and financial challenges were beginning to manifest themselves in New Jersey, with production of new projects stalled. Even so, Brenon managed to continue his policy of attracting big names from the theatre, into his films. He collaborated with the noted stage actor Sir Johnston Forbes Robertson, on a film version of *The Passing of the Third Floor Back*. The actor's portrayal of the character of "the stranger" was well established and it was an intriguing project for Brenon to have undertaken. It was shot at his studio in New Jersey.

A large boarding house, on three floors with seventeen rooms was constructed. "Two months were spent in filming the story of the changes wrought in the lives of the mean-spirited and scheming members of the gloomy Bloomsbury lodging house, by the mysterious occupant of the third floor back", wrote *Motion Picture News*. Sir Johnston was enthusiastic to have his performance in this play be "given the permanency of celluloid". During the filming, Brenon developed appendicitis and was carted off to hospital. Randolph Bartlett, a friend at *Photoplay* magazine attributed this medical challenge, as the reason the film was completed "without any of his characteristic vigour". Fans of the actor were none too impressed. "It is no more a true representation of Forbes Robertson, than a news-weekly glimpse of President Wilson, is an estimate of the work of our national executive," retorted one American critic. Nonetheless, it has some redeeming features, including evocative moody interiors and some signs of Brenon's talents at the strange and bizarre. It is important, because it remains one of the few examples of Brenon's work, from the time, when he was making films as an independent, in New Jersey.

Brenon planned a number of other productions at his studio, including an adaptation of *Kismet*, but wider challenges with his new enterprise, scuppered these plans. Brenon was paying back significant loans. There was simply not enough revenue generated at the studio, to service them. The Herbert Brenon Film Corporation, also got mired down in a series of lawsuits. There was Jennie Jacobs, who went to court to determine her standing as the owner of twenty five thousand dollars worth of stock in the business. English actor George Arliss (who would later play Disraeli on film) was suing for 22,500 dollars, which he believed was due to him, from an unfulfilled Brenon contract. The most intriguing was the Dancer Dazie, who appeared in a stage production which Brenon had funded. The act had appeared in the Palace theatre, New York for a week, after which it had been relegated to the storehouse. Brenon had invested seven thousand dollars in the production. Its star, Dazie was said to be under contract to Brenon, and was looking for payment. Dazie was also said to be recovering in the countryside, from a nervous disorder, perhaps brought on, by the stress of the cancellation of the show, or his dealings with Brenon. Lewis Selznick, although he owned Brenon Corporation stock, argued to the court, that he had no responsibility, for the contracts entered into by Brenon. Ultimately, however, it was a falling out with his key financier William Bumstead, who called in his loans to Brenon, effectively taking control of the Hudson Heights studios. This marked the end for his studio empire in New Jersey. Arguably, Brenon was not an easy man to do business with, and of course his high profile and sometimes exaggerated sense of his own importance, made him a target for other industry figures, and people who felt, he had trampled on their dreams. Leaving the United States and going to Europe for a time was opportune, and a prestigious project was in the offing. As his friend at *Photoplay* magazine put it, "When everything appeared at its blackest a rainbow burned for Brenon in the Eastern sky. The British government had sent for him, to produce a great patriotic picture for English consumption! "

The British authorities had appointed Lord Beaverbrook, as Minister for Information, and Herbert Brenon was invited by the government and the National War Aims Committee, to take charge of an ambitious propaganda project titled, *Invasion of Britain*, with a script by the popular novelist, Hall Caine. The narrative of Brenon's film, concerned the impact of a German invasion on the people, living in a quintessential, insular, English city. If Germany was to invade Britain, from a visual point of view, it would add to the dramatic statement, if the story had the city of Chester, falling victim to the foreign aggressor. In this scenario, the city would receive the ultimate humiliation, a German governor, installed in this most archetypal of English settings, with its beautiful and distinctive traditional architecture.

In 1918, Herbert Brenon moved into the comfortable Grosvenor Hotel, located in the centre of the city. He felt that he was carrying the world on his shoulders, as he tried to make a film which would prepare the British public for a potential invasion. The film was going to detail, the atrocities that the Germans had been blamed for, during the previous years of the conflict. His sense of the urgency of his mission and the morality of his calling was strong. "Mr. Brenon takes himself seriously, as befits the apostle of propaganda by film, and he has the gift of being taken seriously", observed the *Daily Express*. "He inspires confidence, his memory is infallible, his method, an amalgam of firmness, skill, and good humour. He knows what he wants and gets it done". To those unfamiliar with what was going on, shock was widely reported, as hundreds of

German soldiers, appeared in many of Chester's narrow streets and outside local shops. The soldiers were hostile and well trained, real British soldiers, in German uniform. As a local journalist commented, "Had you been in Chester during the past forthnight you would have thought that the Germans were really here. The old city has been turned upside down and inside out. One man has been in possession. That man is Herbert Brenon. The people and even the military are at his beck and call. He gives an order, and the troops obey. He lifts his hand and a large restless mob becomes a flock of sheep. Even Mark Anthony could not have done better".

Somewhat predictably, Brenon who was not always known for his tact or sensitivity, brought many of his colleagues with him from the United States. This further wounded the pride and ambitions, of the struggling local British film industry, already devastated by the war. The choice of the Irish-American to take charge of the project provoked some criticism. Indigenous British film producers felt that the advances that their own native film industry had made, were being overlooked by the choice of Brenon, an invader, on their territory, so to speak, for this important "national" project. After several weeks filming, either by accident or sabotage, the footage was completely destroyed in a fire in June 1918, at the London film base. The highly emotional Brenon, was now sent into the depths of despair, and only much encouragement from colleagues, made it possible for him, to muster the energy to begin again, and re-shoot.
The film got behind schedule because of the June fire, and in

September 1918, two cast members nearly drowned, during the shooting of a scene. As the *Chester Chronicle* noted, "there seems no end to the vicissitudes of the national film which is being produced by the Ministry of Information". A major sequence took place, in Castle square, and outside Chester town hall. The film schedule vividly described the events;

3am artillery arrives from a neighbouring town: 8.30 sees the arrival of troops from camp ; 8.45 the costuming of German troops; 9 o'clock, the assembling of 1,000 women; 9.30 women with banners marching into Castle Square; 9.45 women dispersed by German cavalry and infantry; 10 o'clock, demonstration by the women ' No Peace without Victory ' scene; 10.30, street scenes, departure of troops; 11 o'clock , German troops with guns assembling in Town Hall Square; 11.30, women dragged out of their homes; 12 o'clock, English Tommies under arrest of German troops; 1pm lunch; 2 o'clock , retreat of the German army while under bombardment of British troops; 4.15 departure of troop train.

The newspapers noted Brenon's "hypnotic influence" over the local women of Chester and his manner of speaking, which was likened to a clergyman, speaking to his flock. Using his large megaphone, he addressed a thousand women gathered in the Town Hall square.

"Women of Chester. Women of England. Listen to every word I say. I want you all, to answer with your hearts as well as your lips.

Would you make munitions for the Germans to kill your sons, your husbands, your lovers? Wouldn't you rather die first".

During the making of the film, Brenon had the pleasure of working with famous names of the English stage."Ellen Terry, bless her heart, came along and did a little sequence for me. I shall never forget those few days as long as I live. What charm, what everlasting youth, what talent, what beauty, what an angel! She bucked me up a whole lot, and the mere fact that she had done her bit encouraged the others". Although, the full details of the narrative were kept largely under wraps, the large scale nature of the production, filmed on location in Chester, attracted significant media attention. In the words of film historian, Kevin Brownlow, *Invasion of Britain*, was "the worst kept secret of the war". Some of the writing and comments from the British military to the press were incongruous, as if they had "gone Hollywood" themselves, caught up in the excitement of the film process. The film director stretched the patience of the military almost to breaking point, on some occasions. Brenon kept a Lieutenant Chambers, scurrying from London to Chester, and back again every day, locating castles or policemen, when required by the director.

In particular, Captain Starkey had to contend with numerous requests for troops at short notice. One day, Starkey announced to the press, his intention of writing a book on, "the trials and tribulations of a military attaché" to the film project. The experience was emotionally draining for Brenon. He was preparing the British public for a possible German invasion, through the auspices of a relatively new technology and mode of address. Yet, for some reason, providence perhaps, conspired against the film's timely completion. A usually enthusiastic and inveterate letter writer, he had remained low key, with his foreign correspondence. He finally broke his silence, by communicating with a young, Louella Parsons, in October 1918. At this time, Louella was working as a columnist for the New York *Morning Telegraph*, and Brenon kept her up to date, with his progress on his important work in Britain. Of course with Brenon, there is an underlying humour, always at work. "I came here very quietly, as you know, quite unheralded. One does not wish to advertise the fact that one is doing national work. While I consider it the crowning honour of my career that I should have been invited over here to do this work I also realize the very great sense of responsibility; there were many messages from this war to the world, and if I could but bring home one of these to the masses I would have done a little bit, so I came. On the boat I imagined that the whole army and navy, indeed, the entire civic population would assist me. I had not been here one week before I realized that I was the one that had to fight... I was quite a stranger, the high officials of the government were beginning to realize the importance of the motion picture camera as a great demonstrator of propaganda, but the under officials scorned it. I gave up officialdom for a while and spent a few days with Sir Hall Caine... We went over the story together; we made up our minds we would see it through no matter what happened, and we went ahead".

Brenon's own modus operandi suggested a level of extravagance, which the British government could have done without. The historian Rachael Low, in her history of the British film, would describe much of the problems with the production of *Invasion of Britain* as being caused by Brenon's "leisurely style". In a time of peril, and austerity, someone less lavish and egocentric at the helm, might have helped. But, the British government had chosen a filmmaker of exceptional ability, someone capable of making a big impact, onscreen and off. Brenon expected that many of his projects would require substantial resources, and had to be made in a certain way. Therefore, there is no sense that Brenon was acting uncharacteristically, or in bad faith, on *Invasion of Britain*. Indeed, if the fire had not occurred in June, 1918, destroying so much footage, the film, in all likelihood, would have been completed before the end of the war. The production was now irrelevant and was never shown. It came up for discussion at a parliamentary committee meeting in Westminster, after the war. Later the British Treasury, ordered all copies of the film, to be destroyed. Although no complete copy remains, a sepia toned fragment of the film exists (screened to the author by the film historian, Kevin Brownlow at his offices, at Photoplay Productions, in London). This material features armoured vehicles on the move in the English countryside, scenes in Chester, and a poignant, impressive interior sequence, featuring Ellen Terry. The spectacular crowd scenes are missing, but even these remaining film fragments, indicate how interesting and important the project was, and the care that Brenon had taken.

The Star

Herbert Brenon was relieved that the war was at an end, just as he had been profoundly moved by what he had seen on the western front. He was among a select number of civilians, given permission to visit the war zone by the British government. Now, paradoxically, after the shelving of *Invasion of Britain*, he was unsure what to do next. He went back to America briefly, for Christmas 1918, but was in a strange sombre mood. He was exhausted from his extensive work on a project, which seemed so important, but was now redundant. In the United States, he had secured American citizenship, but as he surveyed the film industry, he was surprised by some of the changes that had occurred in this short time. He also had the debts of the Brenon Corporation hanging over him, and thought it wise to base himself in Europe, for a bit longer. He received an offer from Edward Godal, who ran a British film company called B and C films, to direct some projects. Brenon was now showing off his star, Marie Doro, in the tearooms of the Savoy Hotel, London, in February 1919. The actress, a native of Duncannon, Pennsylvania, had first come to prominence in theatre before making films with the Famous Players Company. Brenon would enjoy a close collaboration with her. He had always been attracted to intelligent actresses, who had strong views, but who ultimately succumbed to his charms and direction. Doro was intelligent and thoughtful, and the pair got on well together.

He was offering words of encouragement to British film production, telling the *Daily Express*, that it had "a great future". At this time, his Ministry of Information escapade now complete, he was moving on. "The taste for sensationalism on the film is gradually disappearing. The merely spectacular photo-drama is also doomed. The public wants plays of live human interest". The first of the films for B and C was to be titled, *Twelve-Ten*, a mystery thriller for all intents and purposes to be filmed in England and France. Brenon had always been vocal on the multifaceted skills needed for his role. "The director must be an executive, a dramatist, an author, a leader of men and a painter. He must be a painter, or possess artists' qualities, because a photoplay is never action alone; it is always, in part, a picture".

Twelve: Ten opens on a shot of a clock. Then the image fades out. The film introduces Louis Fernandez, "once an actor, now a struggling sculptor of Montmartre" and his daughter Marie (Marie Doro). Father and daughter are seen taking a trip in an open topped carriage, through Paris. While on route the sculptor shows his daughter a new miniature, which he is bringing to the city, to try to sell to Francoise, a Parisian art dealer. The next scene reveals that a wealthy English manufacturer, Lord Chatterton, is currently on a sojourn in Paris. At the premises of Francoise, the sculptor is endeavouring to impress the art dealer with his latest work, which the latter describes as unoriginal. The sculptor is upset, and leaves the premises with his daughter. The discussion has been overheard, by the elderly businessman, who is moved by the scene, and asks Francoise, for the address of the sculptor. Later, Marie and her father stop for a drink, at a cafe. She begs her depressed father not to drink alcohol. While sitting at a table, they are approached by a gypsy, who offers to tell Marie's fortune. "I see you Mademoiselle, rich- noble- in a beautiful home", the fortune-teller, informs her. In conversation with the gypsy, Marie has forgotten about her father, and now cannot seem to locate him. Not far from the scene, Lord Chatterton witnesses the sculptor jump off a nearby bridge. He takes Marie away in his carriage, later to inform her of the tragic event. The young girl comes to live in England, at his home. It is a world far removed from the penury existence in Paris, and Marie has to get used to her surroundings, to the butler, and Lord Chatterton's entourage. He has a busy life, at his industrial premises, Port Chatterton, the foundation of his millions. Marie visits him often at work, sometimes to the annoyance of his employees, who are not certain of the young woman's status, in their employer's life. The business faces a number of challenges, not least, problems with some of the personnel. When financial bonds of considerable value go missing, the staff are under suspicion.One evening, after a game of chess, Lord Chatterton, falls ill and dies. In a dramatic and effective sequence the family and key members of the firm are gathered together, as the will is read out. Chatterton's estate is left to his newly adopted daughter, Marie. The tension is built up wonderfully, and the film keeps the attention of the viewer. The point of view shots in *Twelve-Ten*, the elaborate building up of suspense were all hallmarks of Brenon's directorial style. One is concerned for Marie's welfare, as she makes her lonely journey to Chatterton's country castle estate, to pay her last respects, in a bizarre ritual, which he has requested in his will. "No funeral ceremony, no flowers, no mourners. Just my little girl alone, a silent prayer".

At this time, notwithstanding, his words of "encouragement" Brenon discounted France or Britain, as serious challengers, in a world beginning to be dominated by the American cinema. Both countries bore the scars of the Great War. Having originally blazed a trail with the pioneering work of Louis Lumiere and George Melies, France was showing evidence of being slow to adopt new production practices, and weak at getting the investment community, to row in behind film production. The consequences were plain to see, with hundreds of American films shown in French theatres. Britain was also hampered, in Brenon's view by its climate and excessive caution on the part of investors. In addition, Britain had few stars, because producers did not pay actors enough to enable them to concentrate on movies in a full-time capacity.

Before the First World War, the cinema had been dominated by France and Italy. After the war, America was in the ascendancy, with much of Europe's traditional foreign markets for films, in South America and elsewhere, taken over by the aggressive marketing and distribution of American films, in these territories, during the war. The *Moving Picture World* noted. "Men who are deservedly considered experts in export trade and government bureaus and organizations, whose business it has been to promote our foreign commerce have declared that the European conflict will place American manufacturers far in the lead in the neutral markets of the world, and after the war will place us in a much more favourable position for the exchange of commodities with most of the belligerents".

Still, Brenon admired the pre-war history of Italian film-making and the achievements of early epic films, like *Quo Vadis* (1913) and *Cabiria* (1914). He observed that the Italians could make films for a fifth, of what it would cost in America. The Italian scenery and climate were great assets. There was also a culture of creativity and innovation in Italy. The native film industry, though a rival, admired America. The country was keen to learn, constantly studying the films and new techniques pioneered in the United States. Equally important, Union Cinematographica Italiana, had been established and the banks were investing heavily in the business, and in theatre chains. When Herbert Brenon was invited by Signor Barattolo, President of UCI, to make films in Italy, to promote Italian film production internationally, he took the opportunity of doing so. He was also able to collect information, on what he saw, of the progress of the Italian film industry.

In Italy, Brenon surveyed the scene. Surprised by what he saw, he concluded that it was unrealistic to assume that the innate artistry of Americans, was going to convincingly trump the artistry of Italians, on a global level. The larger market for movies in the United States helped, but Brenon did not believe that it would be enough, unless American producers also considered the world, when choosing subject matter and themes. His own film work was a testament to that approach. Even today it represents the prototype of what much of the American cinema became. Versions of *Les Miserables*, *Dr Jekyll and Mr. Hyde*, *Robin Hood* running around in *Ivanhoe*, various spy capers shot in foreign lands, desert adventures, fantasy films for the family, and mythical narratives, perhaps, of mermaids and exotic creatures, off the Bermuda and Jamaica coasts.

However, this prescient sense of Italy remaining one of the dominant forces in the cinema, was yet another of Brenon's intelligent insights. Italy's national cinema, would become one of the most influential in the world, with its famous names like Federico Fellini, Roberto Rossellini and Michelangelo Antonioni. Furthermore, it is hard to imagine an American cinema, anything but impoverished, without the influence of Italian American directors, like Francis Ford Coppola, or the maker of the brilliant *Hugo*, Martin Scorsese. In 1920, Brenon instinctively felt the Italians were doing everything to try to bridge the gap with America. "Italy has watched our methods, copies them, and improves on them. I believe she will lead us, if we are not careful. America has only one competitor – Italy".

The Mysterious Princess, was Brenon's first Italian project, based on his own original story and screenplay. Princess Marietta of Turania (Marie Doro) is orphaned when her parents are killed by republican rebels. She seeks refuge on an island, with the help, of the kindly Prime minister. The rebels find her, but she makes her escape with the assistance of a young writer, Jack Merton. The Princess goes on a journey to Venice. She is in disguise, dressed as a boy, pretending to be Merton's servant, to evade the pursuing rebels. She is finally captured by the rebels, but is freed by Merton. The Prime minister subdues the rebels, and offers her the throne, but the Princess turns her back on a life of royalty, to instead, live a simple life with Merton. Brenon made the five reel film in Rome, Venice and Naples, and on the island of Capri. He enjoyed filming in Italy, in the company of Marie Doro. "Venice! Oh, the motion picture beauty of the spot, with its old buildings, black gondolas, curved bridges, churches, pigeons, piazzas, odd ceremonies and countless other glories. The Mediterranean! Every town breathing art and temperament, and every mountain and river praying to be photographed and painted", he enthused. The film encompassed, in its exuberant atmosphere, outdoor settings, complex logistics, and heavy emphasis on action and romance, many of the ingredients that would define the archetypal, commercially orientated feature film.

"The setting, needless to say, is a thing of beauty", wrote the *Times* of London, "for liberal use has been made of some of the most delightful spots in Venice and on the Island of Capri. The acting is quite good, but the story is wildly impossible. The mystery about the heroine is why ferocious conspirators, masked and hooded, should be so anxious to kidnap her on every possible occasion, to pursue her among the caves of Capri, to dash after her in swift Motor-boats – which must have been an absolute terror to the other users of the canals of Venice – and to threaten her with death when they do at last succeed in capturing her".

During the making of *Beatrice* (1920) (a narrative, from the famous British author of adventure stories, Sir Rider Haggard) a quite separate story, became international news.

The *New York Times* reported that Brenon had vanished, "four days ago while taking scenes with an Italian company. It is said he left for a walk during a luncheon rest on Mount Etna and did not return. Great anxiety is felt for him on account of the snow on the precipitous cliffs". What followed in a number of the papers was a recount of Brenon's career highlights, including reference to his recent work for the British government, as the American journalists prepared to write the obituary, of a filmmaker, whose star had shone so brightly. As the story unfolded, it was revealed that there had been a series of kidnappings in the Sicilian area, in an effort to extort money, but to date they had kidnapped locals, not foreign nationals. This represented a sinister new departure. On January 14, 1920, the situation was resolved and the film director was located. He had been the victim of brigands, (perhaps) who had taken him to a deserted monastery, some 14 miles away, where he had been robbed of his money and other valuables. Later, he was released unhurt, but apparently forced to make the long walk back. The *New York Times* suggested that he was released, when he was found to be an American.

Norma

In 1921, Herbert was back in America and soon becoming a well-known figure in the life of Gotham at this time, serving on the art committee of New York's, civic club and regularly attending exhibitions and functions at the Metropolitan Museum of Art. He was the complete artist, in many respects, talking of literature and painting, sculpture and music. He was interested in Russian cinema, and what became known as the German expressionist films of the 1920s, best represented by *The Cabinet of Dr. Caligari*. He showed a keen interest in early writings on the cinema. He was fond of quoting Hugo Munsterberg, (author of *The Photoplay: A Psychological Study*) and poet and theorist Vachal Lindsay, in his efforts, to show how important the cinema was, as an art form. If that was not enough, Brenon could be found at Columbia University, giving some lectures on motion picture production and arguing for the need for Film Education, in the United States. His views about America had matured, and he no longer saw the country as the clichéd land of opportunity. Success in America, he believed, was determined on the extent to which an individual cultivated the imagination. "There, the thought, the plan, the energy, and the success of your labours are measured, in no small degree, by your originality". He was based at 318 East 48th Street, in New York.

Joseph Schenck, producer and agent, had recently married the actress Norma Talmadge, and had set up a company to make film vehicles, for his new wife. Schenck, who would later become head of United Artists and Twentieth Century Fox, was enthusiastic about the Brenon connection. "It gives me exceptional satisfaction to make this announcement of Mr. Brenon's affiliation with me. In no other way could I give a better assurance of my earnestness in promising bigger and better productions for 1921. I consider Herbert Brenon, a great artist".

Brenon was working with the Tipperary born screenwriter Mary Murillo, at this time. She seems to have been a dynamic character. She had a career in the early American cinema and later in Britain and France. She first came to notice in the Chorus line of the musical Havana on Broadway. Very few stage opportunities followed but she began writing scenarios and sending them into the film studios for consideration. In *The Sign on the Door*, adapted by Murillo, Ann Hunniwell (Norma Talmadge) accompanies Frank Devereaux (Lew Cody) to a New York cafe, and ends up arrested during a raid, and has her picture taken by a newspaper photographer, leading to a serious of interweaving events. Brenon was working at a frenetic pace. By day he was directing scenes for *The Sign on the Door*, and by night he was in the cutting room, supervising the editing of, *The Passion Flower*. The time and effort he put into the latter film, including a trip to Chicago, to see the play version, proved worthwhile. As the *Moving Picture World* noted, in its review, "Norma Talmadge gives vivid impersonation in Spanish story of lust and murder".

The Wonderful Thing, was the story of a young woman, who is the daughter of an American hog raiser, who is exceptionally rich from money amassed in the mid-west, who falls for a titled English gentleman. The film was scripted by Brenon and Clara Beranger from the play by Lillian Trimble Bradley and Forrest Halsey. *Variety* noted that, "the role is a relatively light one for Miss Talmadge, being mostly comedy, with a smattering of emotional display". Still, the *Washington Times*, felt that it was, "a fascinating romance of a beautiful young heiress" and that "Miss Talmadge has probably never had a more congenial role than that of the young bride". Brenon also cast a New York socialite in this film, by the name of Julia Hoyt, and she was rare in her willingness to criticise Brenon. "I went into pictures full of hope and enthusiasm, believing that I would be allowed to develop whatever talent I possessed. I wanted to start unheralded and unnoticed and succeed. Instead I was relegated to the fashion-plate field... I soon discovered that to obey instructions implicitly, to be perfect marionettes, was the road to success in the studios. It is not a question of initiative, of characterisation, or of even thinking for yourself. All the thinking is done for you".

A survey conducted at 5,000 movie theatres in the United States by *Moving Picture World*, confirmed that Norma Talmadge was the most popular actress in the country. The press made much of the new film association, with Norma Talmadge, some even suggesting, that Brenon was now permanently connected professionally, with the actress. The domineering Norma, (who Billy Wilder used as a template for his Norma Desmond character, in *Sunset Boulevard*) soon envisaged Brenon, as her director, for all her future films! However, the working partnership with Norma only lasted for three films; *The Passion Flower*, *The Wonderful Thing* and *The Sign on the Door*. (The three films are preserved in the film collection, of the Library of Congress, in Washington.)

Herbert Brenon resided in a country that was conservative, and his films on themes of adultery and transgressions, did not play well outside of the urban centres. America remained very insular and religious, and the influence of the Methodists and the Temperance movement, were gaining momentum. Not all the publicity for Brenon at the time was of the positive variety. The eighteenth amendment to the United States constitution gave legal force to prohibition and it was the law from 1920 to 1933. One evening in New York, in May 1921, a patrolman sighted a man standing in a doorway, on West Forty-Sixth Street. He saw the man hurl a package to the sidewalk and run down the street. The policeman followed in pursuit. After a short chase, he caught the man by the arm and arrested him. The man was later identified as Herbert Brenon, motion picture director. The policeman told the court that he was sure that Brenon had thrown a bottle of Scotch whiskey to the ground. The image of one of America's top directors running away from a pursuing New York policeman may have been the stuff of films, but was considered at the very least to be ignoble to many Americans at the time. However, fortunately for Brenon, the magistrate dismissed the case.

But other stories put Brenon's embarrassment into perspective. The early 1920s were a time of transformation in the film industry. New York was still a key centre, but Hollywood was beginning to become a major focus of production activity. Many settled in very well, but those who moved out West had to depend on themselves, to a greater extent for an order and discipline, which it was much easier to attain, in a well-structured metropolis, like New York – where the film industry could never be the only show in town, or the only topic of conversation. In September 1921, the popular comedian and actor Roscoe Arbuckle, (for many years represented by Joseph Schenck) took a break from filming, and went on a short trip to California, in the company of two other men. They stayed at the St. Francis Hotel, and sometime later, decided to have a party, and invited several women to their suite. One of the young women, Virginia Rappe, became seriously ill that evening, and died in hospital, several days later. Roscoe was accused by another partygoer of having raped Virginia, and in the course of this act, rupturing her bladder.

During the course of several trials, the media was flooded with salacious stories about the American film industry. Arbuckle was exonerated, but the scandal destroyed his career. When the dust began to settle on this troubling episode, the industry was shaken by another major incident. The well-known Hollywood film director, also with an Irish lineage, William Desmond Taylor, was found murdered in his home, in Bungalow court, in Los Angeles, on February 2, 1922.

The more the L.A. police delved, the murkier the story became. The case was never solved. The industry which had prided itself on respectability and which had cultivated a very clean veneer, was now associated with the very opposite. Brenon was quick to see the dangers and spoke out almost immediately, as one of the leading filmmakers in America. "I shudder when I think of this Taylor murder and the conditions which it suggests. The industry is bound to suffer as a result. Just as it received a setback after the Arbuckle case, so it will receive another setback now, and people all over the country will regard such happenings at Hollywood as representative of the entire moving picture industry, which they are not. The trouble is that out in Hollywood the motion picture people are thrown upon themselves for recreation. They live, think and talk pictures all the time. The minority, who have made money quickly, persons with little character and less morals, have had their heads turned and have cast aside all restraint. These are the ones who bring discredit upon us, and the good suffer with the bad. It is segregation which has made Hollywood what it is – turned it from a place famous as a centre of the motion picture industry into a place notorious as a centre of vice".

Brenon, in retrospect, appears astonishingly callous. There are no words of sadness, to be found at the demise of a colleague. Even by Hollywood standards, Brenon appears shockingly cold. The main concern is public perception about the film industry, although not everyone agreed with his analysis. In particular, Carl Laemmle rejected any criticism of Hollywood, describing it as a healthy place to live and work. In the 1920s, the papers reported the two very different opinions on Hollywood, the positive view from Carl Laemmle – and the more suspicious and negative view that Brenon held. However, Brenon's view of Hollywood as shady and underhand was shared by many actors and actresses, who felt vulnerable, and did not want to go out to work there. Brenon's attitude to some aspects of the insular Hollywood lifestyle continued to be critical, for many years, and affected the perception of Los Angeles, by other creative people.

Brenon's former colleague, William Fox, was still in business and now controlled 800 film theatres in America. Fox directors of the 1920s, included Raoul Walsh and John Ford. Herbert made a decision to return, to make films with the man who the press, not too long ago, had considered his arch nemesis. By now, Brenon had developed a clear sense of his own identity. He was a film director, but also a literary Irishman, who stressed the importance of story and screenplay, and who would have been an influence on other ambitious directors, like John Ford. At the Fox studios, Brenon worked with the actress Pearl White, directing her in *Any Wife*. She would describe Brenon as, "the one and only real picture director in the whole comic business". Another production at this time, and Brenon's only Western, was *Moonshine Valley*, based on a story from Mary Murillo which featured William Farnum and Sadie Mullen, in the lead roles. It was full of action scenes, including two notable fights between Farnum and the

actor Holmes Herbert. It was the start of the career of actress Dawn O'
Day, aged three years of age. Jean, the famous moving picture dog, also
featured in the film. "The fact that Herbert Brenon directed the picture is
the best assurance that *Moonshine Valley* is a photoplay out of the ordinary
run of moving pictures, this director being noted for his human touches and
startling effects" stated the *Pullman Herald*.

The breadth of Brenon's interests during this second phase with Fox was
evident in a variety of eclectic material, including *A Stage Romance*, a
biographical film about the great English stage actor, Edmund Kean. In the
early 19th century Kean had held audiences enthralled at Drury Lane,
London, as Shylock in The Merchant of Venice and in Richard III, and had
followed up with rave attention and later bitter controversy on his tours of
America, (due to his prodigious drinking and a widely publicised extra-
marital affair). *A Stage Romance* was a film with impressive settings and
costumes and William Farnum was effective as the great Edmund Kean. A
special screening of the film took place at the annual party of the Cinema
Composers Club of Columbia University (at the Japanese Garden) in April
1922. This second interlude with William Fox was not without some
modest achievements. Still, it was far from the ideal studio for Herbert
Brenon. It was 1923. The film industry was highly competitive, it was
something of a coup for Paramount, to get the larger than life Herbert
Brenon, to join them.

He had dazzled the cinema world before the First World War, and it was reasonable to assume he could do so again, yet many other prominent directors of that era, including D.W. Griffith, were rapidly fading from view. Could Brenon be a major figure of the 1920s, and capture film audience expectations, as he had successfully done in the past? For Paramount, only time would tell. The temperamental Irishman, was certainly going to be difficult to manage, as the studio had found to its cost with another of the silent greats.

"Brenon was at least as inflexible as Griffith", American film historian, Richard Koszarski, would write, "an Irish curmudgeon who was prone to giving interviews denouncing studio interference and upholding the status of artists like himself". In many ways, though, it was a perfect match. Paramount was a studio with significant resources, and its founders Adolph Zukor and Jesse Lasky exceptional entrepreneurs, who were on a mission to build up a cinema empire from modest beginnings. The founders of Paramount, had distributed films featuring the celebrated French actress Sarah Bernhardt and had certain lofty ambitions. Brenon was debonair and sophisticated, speaking fluent French, talking of fine wines, pretty women, and well versed in all the music and literature of the day. The studio had competent in-house producers, like William Le Baron, Walter Wanger and B.P. Schulberg, managing day to day production operations, out of Paramount's New York studios, and at their other production base, in Hollywood. *The Rustle of Silk* (1923) was Brenon's first film for the studio, based on a novel by Cosmo Hamilton. Brenon brought his own background, his English private education, the British newspaper and society world of his Irish born parents and the unfulfilled ambitions of his father for a career in politics, at the Westminster parliament, to the story. In, *The Rustle of Silk*, a love triangle develops between a British Member of Parliament, Arthur Fallaray (Conway Tearle) his wife, Lady Feo (Anna Q. Nilsson) and a maid Lola (Betty Compson) who comes to work in the household. At first Arthur's wife is too busy to notice, events in her midst, preferring the company of a British newspaper owner played by Cyril Chadwick. Letters reveal the relationship between Arthur and Lola. She confesses, but persuades Arthur to stay in politics. Benefitting from Lola's discretion, he eventually becomes British Prime Minister. The film attracted some attention. *Los Angeles Times* noting that, "Miss Nilsson has seldom been more handsomely decked with gowns, and Miss Compson, even though she is poor, wears several elaborate creations." *Photoplay* was more supportive of Brenon. "There are at least several instances of directorial excellence. His scenes in and about the London Ritz are carefully handled. So too, are the difficult Parliament shots. And there are many flashes revealing the mental processes of his characters".

The Woman with Four Faces starred Betty Compson and Richard Dix. The narrative of a complex female crook who outwits the police and who also steals the heart of the District Attorney. It was a film which the Russian filmmaker, Eisenstein, was said to have admired. At Paramount, Brenon tended to deal directly with Jesse Lasky, the Vice-President, in charge of production. As Thomas Schatz has noted in, *The Genius of the System*, the higher the budget and the more prestigious the project, the less Paramount interfered, leaving their top Producer/Directors to get on with making their films largely unhindered. Intense discussions would take place with Jesse Lasky and centre on script, casting and budget approval. Once these issues were agreed, Brenon was left on his own with the freedom to make his films as he saw fit. William Le Baron, would often act as the Associate Producer of the Herbert Brenon productions, for Famous Players Lasky / Paramount. The studio boss, Jesse Lasky was very supportive of Brenon, and it was the beginning of a fruitful creative partnership.

Brenon's reputation for imaginative direction, humour and craftsmanship became firmly established at Paramount with films like, *The Spanish Dancer* (1923), filmed in Los Angeles. The romance of a gypsy girl in Spain, during the reign of Philip IV, it was an ambitious epic costume drama, with actress Pola Negri, and Antonio Moreno. It was based on the play, Don Cesar de Bazan, and was adapted by June Mathis. Mathis had also collaborated with Irish director Rex Ingram, *on The Four Horsemen of the Apocalypse* (1921) made for Metro Studios. *The Spanish Dancer* was the start of a memorable and successful collaboration, between Brenon and cinematographer, James Wong Howe. During the preparatory work, much focus was paid to the script and storyboarding of the movie. The screenplay held in the Paramount production files at the Academy of Motion Picture Arts and Sciences in Los Angeles, shows a clever structure and Brenon's trademark attention to detail. Brenon's moving picture star, Pola Negri, had a reputation for high living, eccentric behaviour and exoticness. She had a white Rolls Royce and a chauffeur.

Her life was one party after another, followed by a temperamental outburst. If his exciting star had a reputation, as a fiery personality, Brenon put this in context. "Pola Negri is temperamental, but she has her temper under tight control. An actor without temperament is like a violin without strings. You can't play on either one of them". Nonetheless, the filming was somewhat tense, and Pola would later describe working with him unfavourably. "A volatile and fastidious man who insisted that things be done his way", and she remembered that there were, "many flare-ups, that often held up work for an entire day".

The cast also featured Wallace Beery, Adolphe Menjou and young Dawn O'Day. The child actress was achieving much success, and would later change her name to Anne Shirley, to match the character in the classic story, *Anne of Green Gables*. The exquisite detail of *The Spanish Dancer*, the sets, the costumes, the dresses, all show the Brenon attention to a lush mise en scene. Brenon had a brilliant eye for composition and he was a director who challenged his crew to be ambitious. He sought to enable the spectators, to fully inhabit his cinematic world. He was skilful at supervising the editing of his films. He also had much to say about the dialogue titles and descriptive titles, often humorous, which were so much a part of the silent era. *The Spanish Dancer* was the subject of a new distribution strategy, the first of Paramount's films to be released simultaneously, on the East and West coast, opening on the 4 November, 1923. If Paramount had ample resources to take on elaborate projects, the studio was also tolerant of the director's emotional and excitable outbursts, as well as his varied interests. This included Brenon's manner of playing the stock market, in between takes, at New York's Paramount Astoria Studio, which astonished many visitors, particularly the diehard thespians.

For, *The Side Show of Life* (1924) a beautiful circus set was built in New York. A tattooed man, a snake charmer, a leopard, an entire family of lions, all added to the realistic atmosphere. Unfortunately, a baby lion cub, proved difficult to control, during filming. It objected, when The Marseillaise was played on a hand organ! *The Side Show of Life* starred Ernest Torrence, as an English clown, who somewhat unlikely becomes a Brigadier-General, during the war. Torrence, a graduate of the Royal Academy of Music, had given up an operatic career for acting. In America since 1911, he had a successful career on Broadway, before ending up in films, where he frequently played menacing characters. But, this was a more subtle role for him. In the film, the war is just a memory, as the soldier returns to his previous job as a juggler, but is no longer able to perform. He moves away from his long time vaudeville partner, Elodie (Louise Lagrange) but finds love with a new woman, Lady Auriol (Anna Q. Nilsson). Loss, self-sacrifice, loyalty are all issues that Brenon deals with, in poignant and thoughtful narratives. It was among a number of films, directed by Brenon, where the impact of the Great War, is explored through characters that have experienced it directly. It is the social and psychological aspects of war, and its aftermath, that seem to interest him, and which dictates his approach to these films.

The Breaking Point (1924) marked a collaboration with the Irish actor, Matt Moore, one of a trio, of celebrated acting brothers from county Meath. Moore plays Judson Clark, who like Noah in *The Long Strike*, loses some of his cognitive functions, so to speak, when he believes he has committed a murder. More specifically, he believes that he has killed the husband of his lover. He retreats in a blizzard to an isolated cabin, where he almost dies. He recovers his mental wellbeing, somewhat, but has forgotten this memory, locked, in his subconscious, where it remains for ten years. Brenon offered an explanation for the title of the film. "When the mind is taxed to 'The Breaking Point', one of two things must happen. Suicide is one way, and the other is nature's own way of taking care of the mind. It is a brain revolution that drives all memory of what caused the trouble back into the sub-conscious and keeps it there". Brenon, was an ambitious director, fascinated by psychology, enchanted by the early work of Freud, and excited about how film could explore altered states, in complex ways.

The director liked to film on location, but it was also where the greater challenges lay, particularly keeping a project on schedule. *The Alaskan* was the story of a man growing up in the gold rush days of 1898 Alaska, watching capitalists destroy and strip the country of its natural resources. The film starred Thomas Meaghan, Anna May Wong and Estelle Taylor. Brenon's interest in landscape and the natural world, achieved full reign here. Brenon and James Wong Howe experimented with the new panchromatic film stock, achieving more natural exterior results on location in Alaska and British Columbia. *Washington Post* described some of the sequences as, "awe inspiring outdoor views". Elsewhere during filming near Lake Tahoe, the production team were waiting around for heavy snow and shooting was suspended. Brenon was relaxed, but the money conscious Paramount got jittery and ordered large volumes of salt to be delivered to the location, in lieu of snow. The salt was placed on the roofs of the houses and in the specially designed village. But as Paramount's Vice President, Jesse Lasky would later recall (citing this incident), when you start trying to save money in the film business, it often ends up costing you even more. The snow came and remained for miles around except on the exterior village set where it was needed. Herbert Brenon and James Wong Howe arrived the next morning and could do nothing but laugh, observing the effect of the salt on the snow. It is understood that Jesse Lasky also laughed, several decades later.

Directing Peter Pan and The Street of Forgotten Men

When Herbert Brenon entered Adelphi Terrace, London, to meet with Sir J.M. Barrie to discuss the first film adaptation of *Peter Pan*, he knew that he was walking onto a street, which had boasted so many interesting inhabitants, since the days when the theatrical impresario, David Garrick, resided on the street of beautiful, neoclassical designed houses. From the windows, on a clear day, you could see the Houses of Parliament. On one visit, George Bernard Shaw, also a resident at Adelphi Terrace, strolled by on the street below. Brenon remarked on how different the two writers were, describing Barrie as the optimist and Shaw as the pessimist and cynic, but Sir James did not concur. For two decades, the popular fantasy had enthralled and excited audiences around the world; both as a play and in Barrie's subsequent novels *Peter and Wendy* and *Peter Pan in Kensington Gardens*. The film director was on a journey to make a film for Paramount which could, in essence, be enjoyed by all the family, and he wanted a clearer understanding from Sir James, of exactly who Peter was, and what motivated the central character. When the playwright bluntly responded, that Peter was a boy who died the day he was born, the usually exuberant Irish director, something himself, of a poster boy for American ingenuity and positivity, was quickly silenced. Noticing Brenon's vacant visage, a more whimsical J.M. Barrie responded in a gentler manner, even if realism was still far from his mind. The story was about a boy who ran away from home the day he was born, and who subsequently had adventures with a girl called Wendy and her brothers, as well as Indians and Pirates, in Neverland. J.M. Barrie, thus providing the synopsis of the famous story, that Brenon and Paramount were seeking. When they dined, the playwright's manservant attended to them, but few words were spoken. However, even during the significant lapses of conversation that often occurred, at no time did the filmmaker feel anything, but completely at ease with J.M. Barrie. "I have never met any man who charmed me so quickly and completely as did Sir James", Brenon would later recall. " And I have never talked with an author who is so liberal in his views concerning the adaptation of one of his own literary efforts. He was willing to co-operate and open to reason". The playwrights London home contained gifts from George Bernard Shaw, H.G. Wells and Arthur Conan Doyle. When Brenon enquired which of his souvenirs was most precious to him, Barrie opened a drawer, to reveal the key to Kensington gardens, which he had received from King Edward. The making of *Peter Pan* was complicated by Brenon's own dogmatic personality, and a certain prescriptiveness, on the part of J.M. Barrie. When Brenon spoke about the latest gadgets and technology that would be used to make the film, Sir James looked threateningly at the film director. "Remember Brenon, there are no telephones nor automobiles in Peter Pan", he warned. The film director tasked screenwriter, Willis Goldbeck, (also a collaborator with Rex Ingram and John Ford) to work on the adaptation, under Brenon's close supervision. As Brenon would often remark, "no photoplay can endure which hasn't a masterful story as its basis". The screenplay from the 1924 film, held at the Margaret Herrick Library, at the Academy of Motion

Picture Arts and Sciences in Los Angeles, shows a highly polished version of the story, deftly structured for the cinema screen. In theatrical style, J.M. Barrie also insisted that the role of Peter was to be played by a girl. This was not going to be easy, or conventional. Now the challenge was to find the girl to play Peter. Famous names at the studio, including actresses Marion Davies, Gloria Swanson and Lillian Gish all wanted the part. Brenon was under intense pressure, but favoured casting an unknown. Advertisements were taken out in newspapers, and auditions were organised nationwide. It was a movie search not equalled in scale or scope, until David O. Selznick's epic quest for Scarlett O' Hara, in the 1930s, for *Gone with the Wind*.

The culmination of the process was a somewhat comical, but moving event. The two celebrated men of stage and screen, journeyed to a small projection room, in Wardour Street, London, to view the various tests, in order to find the right girl to play the fun loving, adventurous, but delicate boy. Sir James pointed to an actress in the third test, and asked if the director had paid much attention or noticed her. But Brenon was deliberately nonchalant, almost evasive. He refused to show his hand, looked disinterested, as he chose to vaguely nudge Barrie, in the direction he wanted. Time passed. The director agreed that, perhaps, it might be worthwhile to look at the test of that girl again. The two men reviewed the footage, "She's Peter Pan", J.M. Barrie declared, and Brenon stood up enthusiastically affirming Barrie's confidence in the unnamed girl.

On 15 August 1924, it was announced in London, that seventeen year old Betty Bronson from Trenton, New Jersey, had won the coveted role. Girls across America and around the world, who had wanted to be Peter Pan, now wanted to be Betty Bronson, and the young actress soon had ardent fans of both sexes. If actor Douglas Fairbanks Jr. was said to have been smitten, writing love letters to her, he only managed to speak to her briefly, as Betty's mother was always in the room next door. Betty took it all in her stride. She considered herself the luckiest girl in the world, to have been chosen to play Peter.

A very pretty brunette, who would have a successful career in the silent and sound era, named Mary Brian, got the part of Wendy. She was eighteen years of age, when she played this famous character, but the studio promoted her as a more innocent sixteen year old. The youngster was interviewed in Brenon's Bungalow in California, while he was recovering from an eye operation, a factor Mary believed, helped secure the part for her. Jack Murphy and Philippe de Lacey were chosen to play her brothers, John and Michael Darling. The part of the Indian Princess, Tiger Lily, friend of Peter Pan, was played by Anna May Wong, who had grown up in Los Angeles, not far from Chinatown. The family owned a laundrette and discouraged Anna's interest in the film business, but she persisted, and after getting some bit parts as a child, left Los Angeles High School, before completing her studies. Brenon cast her in several films, *Peter Pan* and *The Alaskan*, where her performances received critical praise. Anna May Wong, became the first Asian-American film star. Her career is still central to an understanding of the role of Asian-Americans in the Hollywood film industry, and the additional challenges that faced this community as a result of restrictive legal constraints, in that era, in particular. Of course, the grown-ups had to be cast as well, and some arrived in an unlikely, or improbable fashion. The actress Esther Ralston, was called from the set of a Tom Mix Western film, and turned up at Paramount, all dressed up as a cowgirl, guns on her hips, to test for the role of Mrs Darling. Jesse Lasky, Cecil B. De Mille, Ernest Lubitsch and Mary Pickford called by on the first day of filming, to encourage Brenon's young cast. James Wong Howe recalled having great fun working with all the young people on the production, but remarked that Brenon, "came from the theatre" and could be a bit strict with the children. *Peter Pan* was an ambitious fantasy film and the expectations for the production were high. There were intemperate outbursts from Brenon along the way. The challenge of creating the character of Tinkerbell, proved a bone of contention between Brenon and his cinematographer. Brenon was nostalgic for the effect being achieved, through the elaborate use of mirrors, something that harked back to effective, but elaborate, theatrical stagecraft. James Wong Howe, was not enthused at the notion of trying to photograph a character, that was a reflection, and which constantly changed, as it met different surfaces, so he had his work cut out trying to dissuade Brenon. A compromise was reached; a small light was attached to a trout pole. Some Christmas tinsel was placed on the light to reflect it, and give a sense of movement. The light was on a dimmer board, so could be adjusted in intensity, when necessary. Tinkerbell now moved freely. For the close shots of the Tinkerbell character, actress Virginia Brown Faire played the role. The trick miniature effects and the flying effects with Peter and Wendy, devised using hidden wires by Roy Pomeroy, in California.

Jesse Lasky had to depart for Europe, on a search for new book and play acquisitions for Paramount, and he worried that Brenon, given his volatility, might get isolated filming *Peter Pan* in California – away from Brenon's normal comfort zone, at the Astoria studio, in New York. The erudite Lasky asked his secretary to write to Herbert every few days, with news and gossip of Paramount and New York, including news of Wall Street. Herbert never replied to any of these voluminous letters – busy with the production of *Peter Pan* – but returned six months later, Jesse Lasky later recalled, with "his masterpiece". In *Peter Pan*, everything came together to produce memorable results. The scenes in the Darling family home, as Nana prepares the children for bed, the spectacular adventures in Neverland, the imaginative effects with Tinkerbell, the dancing of Peter with his shadow, all splendidly realised. There was so much to marvel at, from the scenes of the Indians in the forest, Peter in his home and the battle on board the Pirate ship, (with a perfectly cast Ernest Torrence as Captain Hook) all immaculately recreated, by an inspired team, under Brenon's great leadership. At no time, did Brenon's commitment to the project waver, and the result still shows to this day, in the print preserved by the George Eastman House Museum, in Rochester, New York. The filmmaker captured the quintessential quality of the play, its Englishness and by the same token its universality. The Christmas party for Paramount in 1924, was held at New York's Plaza Hotel. Most of the attention was on *Peter Pan* and its young star Betty Bronson, as the teenager moved gracefully between the tables of the film executives, and guests at the celebrations. Paramount Pictures, released the film in the United States in 250 theatres, in December 1924. The nationwide release was an enormous success. Five million admissions within the first week. Brenon's young cast won the hearts and minds, of an otherwise cynical, 1920s audience. People warmed to Betty Bronson and Mary Brian. Kevin Brownlow would later remark that, "Herbert Brenon was the ideal man to direct because he worshipped the play and he didn't want to part from it for an instant". Brownlow also observed that "the cast was unusually strong. Tiger Lily was played by the Chinese-American Anna May Wong, George Ali repeated his part of the dog Nana from the stage and Ernest Torrence played the most entertaining Captain Hook anyone had ever seen". The Times of London, noted that "the film rose to the occasion magnificently, and now we have a silent Peter Pan, who is as delicate a creation and as lovable a figure, as the Peter of the stage". The *Irish Times* gave the film a positive review.

"The managers of the Metropole Cinema deserve thanks for bringing the *Peter Pan* film to Dublin promptly, and, still more, for bringing it in the holidays, so that young people may be taken to see it. *Peter Pan* is perhaps the film of the year". In the 1920s, with *Peter Pan*, Brenon explores film form, and the possibilities of opening up filmic space, in an imaginative and captivating manner, which set the bar for the modern fantasy film of later decades. In *Peter Pan*, Brenon continues to surprise in his imaginative use of space, time, editing and décor, to enhance the narrative values of the story. *Time* magazine was full of praise. "The direction of Herbert Brenon gave heart once more to those who still argue that there is imaginative intelligence in the picture industry".

Brenon brought a contradictory force to American cinema. He had an instinctive desire for large set pieces and publicity as well as an undoubted capacity to generate excitement with his films, that we associate with contemporary Hollywood – but also there was a harking back to the days of British and American theatre, where there was room for a personal, low key style of presentation, where serious themes were explored, and the popular expectations of audiences, not necessarily, always fulfilled. Nevertheless, even here, he would use his own status as a film personality, to guide an audience into concluding, that a specific narrative that he was telling, was novel or important. Brenon's reputation was soaring and his significance in America recognised. "When the future history of the screen art is written" noted the *Washington Post*, "it is fairly certain that the name of Herbert Brenon, will be written in capital letters".

Although he reached the height of his creative powers in the 1920s, it is clear that his position in American film history can be said to be established much earlier, if anything adding to his significance. For it is the commitment to the longer film, the star system, the beginning of the development of recognisable film genres which became more clearly defined in the 1920s, and the complex interaction with the public, through a sophisticated use of personal and studio publicity, that sets Brenon out as a pivotal figure, even before the outbreak of the first world war. He was an enigma to most people, but not perhaps to Douglas Fairbanks Jr, who described Brenon as, "a clever caricature of a wildly temperamental movie director". Brenon showed an exceptional ability to identify and support new talent in writing, cinematography and design. He showed uncommon respect for established writers, and sought to work closely with them. He also hoped by doing so, to raise standards in screenwriting in the film industry, by attracting the best writing talent to motion pictures.

If New York's Bowery neighbourhood had once been home to a farm and later stately homes, in the eighteenth century, it quickly descended into urban squalor, by the middle of the nineteenth century. By this time dodgy bars, hoodlums, prostitutes, and gangs, most notably, the Bowery Boys, roamed the space, which had once boasted fine shops and residences. It was capturing the rawness and squalor of this New York neighbourhood, which was one of the challenges facing Brenon, with *The Street of Forgotten Men*. Easy Money Charlie (Percy Marmont) pretends to be disabled, as he makes his living, as a professional beggar on the streets of New York. The film was shot at Paramount's Astoria Studios, and on location, in New York City, vividly re-creating the squalor of the Bowery. Brenon had an affinity with realist authors like Shaw, Ibsen and Honore de Balzac. The filmmaker used a hidden camera, to shoot scenes of beggars on the street, and New Yorkers visiting soup kitchens. "For fine dramatic detail, for unusualness, for giving us a glimpse into a world we never see and into the other sides of characters we simply pass in pity on the streets, *The Street of Forgotten Men* is a photoplay revelation", wrote one contemporary critic. *The Los Angeles Times* would later praise a fight scene in the movie, describing it as scarcely equalled in real life, or on screen. "There have been Sinn Fein riots, Boer uprisings, Mexican revolutions and a lot of other tough scraps in history. Let us add to the collection a recent Bar-room battle staged under the direction of Herbert Brenon, in making *The Street of Forgotten Men*."

The film contained a cameo part for newcomer, Louise Brooks, who found the atmosphere, Brenon's demeanour, and the scene in the barroom, somewhat intimidating. After the filming, Brenon took the beautiful actress to America's most celebrated annual sporting and social event, the Kentucky Derby, which more than made up for his earlier coldness to her. If his life could be described as one of extremes, this was evident, in August 1925, as he proceeded to direct *A Kiss for Cinderella*, another film adaptation of a hit J.M. Barrie stage show, an updated telling of the fairy-tale fantasy, this time set in London, during the First World War. Brenon's struggles to interpret the world around him, and to advance the artistry of the motion picture, had produced some of the most important films of the 1920s, and arguably, this would count as one of them. The film re-united the director with the girl who he had transformed into a huge star, the previous year, Betty Bronson. Playing opposite Bronson was the Irish actor Tom Moore (brother of Matt). Brenon had visited J.M. Barrie to discuss changes in the narrative *of A Kiss for Cinderella* and found the playwright, steadfast in his professionalism and pragmatism. He agreed to make several major changes to the play for the film version, impressing Brenon with his ruthlessness, a quality that Brenon believed would have shocked many a Hollywood screenwriter!

In *A Kiss for Cinderella*, Betty Bronson appears as a young waif in the London of the First World War. She works for little reward cleaning up, in the studio of an artist. When she accidentally triggers a light during an air raid, she attracts the attention and suspicion of a London policeman. A journalist of the time visited the set, and alluded to Brenon's other interests when directing. "A signal came from a man... a man looking remarkably like a successful Wall Street broker who gives some attention to the cut of his clothes, and they stopped acting. The successful Wall Street broker man came over to where we were and was introduced as Herbert Brenon, the director. He, too, was something of a shock. He should have worn at least a bulbous necktie to show he was from the world of art, but he did not. There was not a sign of it anywhere about him". Brenon was also criticised by the journalist for addressing his young star, the eighteen year old Bronson, in an inappropriate manner. When Brenon asked Bronson to shoot the next scene, he casually said, "baby come over here", which angered the journalist, as being disrespectful.

If *Peter Pan* represented a significant advance in film special effects, *A Kiss for Cinderella* (1925) pushed the bar out much further, as mice are turned into horses, and a pumpkin transformed into a dazzling white carriage which carries Bronson over the clouds and crashing through the gates of a magical palace, stopping at the edge of the scene of the palace ball. The film beautifully recreated Cinderella's adventures, with breath-taking ingenuity and skill. "This photoplay is one of sheer delight, a piece as dainty as the finest lace and as welcome as the sea-spray on a midsummer day," wrote the *New York Times*. *A Kiss for Cinderella*, ranks as one of Herbert Brenon's most evocative works. The film is preserved in the collection of the Museum of Modern Art, in New York City.

The Jazz Age and an Adventure in the Desert

The city of New York in the 1920s was experiencing the excitement of Jazz, that unique, but disparate blend of American indigenous music, which had sprouted up in the Southern States, had become popular in cities like Chicago, before changing the New York social scene forever. *Dancing Mothers* (1926), was a Jazz age tale of a mother who initially tries to protect her daughter from an undesirable man, but ends up falling for him herself. The theme of the film was just right for Brenon's sensibilities, the American film industry's veritable, agent provocateur. All the elements came together in this vital drama of modern life, which Brenon made at his favourite location, the Paramount Astoria studios on Long Island. The film director excelled at bringing this intergenerational conflict to life on screen, and he was aided by a highly professional cast. Alice Joyce had entered the film industry through the auspices of Sidney Olcott and the Kalem film company, and was admired for her striking good looks, and sophistication. At the other end of the spectrum, the very pretty Clara Bow, epitomised the 1920s flapper girl. F. Scott Fitzgerald would later describe her as the quintessence of the term "flapper". Essentially young, self-assured girls, with a certain impudence, who were out to have a good time, without stopping to think too much. Young women liked the freedom and liberal air which she represented, while men across America wanted to sleep with her. For Paramount, luring Clara Bow to their studio was to prove, initially, a highly successful move. *Dancing Mothers* focuses on the inappropriateness of Clara's behaviour, constantly smoking, drinking, making telephone calls and jumping up and down on a couch when she is not heading off to nightclubs. This film put her on the map, in the role of the daughter "Kittens". Brenon flirted with Clara during the filming, but he was really closer to Alice Joyce. The film won praise for his imaginative creation of nightclub interiors. It was liked by the young people in the 1920s, who saw in the Jazz age, a unique opportunity for rebelliousness and freedom. As a filmmaker, Brenon is an important chronicler of social mores, changing social patterns, and issues of conformity and non-conformity, in American society. Brenon retained, for the movie, a highly controversial ending. The Alice Joyce character, leaves her carefree daughter Kittens (Clara Bow) and selfish husband behind, to make a new life for herself. It is an important feminist statement. The ending was referred to many times in reviews, including a dire assessment, of how the film would play, outside of the big American cities. Nevertheless, *Variety* considered the movie to be a "beautifully played and generally good picture", and Clara Bow's performance as Kittens, the out of control daughter, "the excellent result of an excellent director". In the director's home town of Dublin, the film censor banned the picture, describing it as, "the sort of filth that led to the necessity for censorship". The film was released on March 1, 1926. It was enthusiastically received by the younger, more liberal sections of the American public, turning Clara Bow, into a star overnight.

There were so many stories Brenon wanted to tell, and new ways to tell them. But when he began discussing an adaptation of P.C. Wren's novel *Beau Geste*, he found colleagues sceptical of the box office potential of the proposed project. Many in the industry considered it foolish, to undertake such a costly enterprise. Films that played heavily on romance were particularly dominant, and females were often the star attraction, even in the desert. But there were few women in the cast of *Beau Geste*. The sales and marketing departments were nervous. How do you sell a film with no romantic interest? The movie was also going to be more expensive to produce than any picture that Paramount had made up to that time. The sheer 'otherness' of the project, three brothers in love with themselves, out in the desert, was a commercial and cinematic challenge.

Brenon was now in his mid-forties, with a wife and grown up son, and was getting tired of the predictability of popular romance films. He believed that he had to argue forcefully for different narratives. After all, if only one kind of love could be shown on the screen, perhaps the critics from the theatre were correct after all. Maybe there was something immature about this new medium of expression. B.P. Schulberg, head of Paramount's West Coast operation tried to dissuade Lasky from proceeding with the project. Lasky countered by insisting that Herbert Brenon and a largely east coast film crew make the movie in California. In addition, the administrative leadership of the east coast Astoria studio went as well, with William Le Baron acting in California, as Paramount's main film executive on the ground, during the filming. Schulberg was furious. This was the vitriolic studio background, and infighting, that Brenon had to cope with, while trying to make *Beau Geste*.

Nothing about this desert adventure was going to be straightforward. But by insisting that the picture be shot on the West Coast, Lasky had at least tempered Brenon's potential to go globetrotting. Ronald Colman was suggested as the lead actor, but was under contract to Sam Goldwyn. The irascible, independent producer, was not about to loan Colman, to any other studio. Finally, an agreement was reached, with Paramount paying 40,000 dollars to secure Colman's services on the film. Neil Hamilton and Ralph Forbes were cast as the brothers, Digby and John. Brenon was confident, that the picture was beginning to take shape. "In more than ten years as a director I have never come across a story that was so well adapted to screen purposes nor have I ever encountered one so filled with fine parts. Any of half a dozen men may dominate the picture. I'm sure I can't tell now. Ronald Colman plays the title role and Neil Hamilton and Ralph Forbes are shown as his younger brothers. It is a toss-up as to which part offers the best possibilities".

The West Coast, offered the opportunity to take advantage of desert terrain, to recreate the North African settings in the story. The key members of the team journeyed from California to nearby Arizona, and into the depths of the Mojave Desert. Glorious sand dunes, some of considerable height, were the vista that unfolded for Brenon and his colleagues. It was rough terrain and this core group travelled on horseback. When they got some miles from Yuma, Brenon found the location he was seeking. The production team arrived, in what looked like a vast deep saucer, or sugar bowl. A beautiful landscape of sand dunes and hills. Brenon had been in difficult terrain before, in Bermuda and Jamaica, but this location in some respects, was more hostile. Coping with the soaring temperatures in the desert would be a major challenge. Water wells would have to be dug. Electricity would have to be provided. A wooden, plank road for transport vehicles, which would stretch for six miles, would need to be constructed. This would only be possible, where the terrain was fairly flat. The last few miles, would still have to be made by cast and crew, on horseback! The Arizona location, which soon came to be called, Camp Brenon, was a world, within a world, for its inhabitants and hundreds of horses and livestock. A city of tents was constructed, including a dining tent to feed two thousand people. A post office, a well producing 50,000 gallons of water daily, which was piped within a few feet of every tent. There were eighty-eight shower baths, an electric lighting system, and a hospital with doctors and nurses. Finally, a tennis court was constructed for Herbert Brenon's amusement! He was paid 2,500 dollars a week for directing the movie. *Photoplay* magazine visited the set and recorded what it saw, "modern science waved its wand and a city of 2,000 men arose from the scorching wilderness of an Arizona desert. Plank roads stretched across the trackless wasteland. Water was coaxed from arid ground. Telephones were conjured by the magic. Electricity bowed to the will of the genii". The military advisor on the film was Lieutenant Louis Van den Ecker, who had served in the French foreign legion and in the Alpine Infantry during the First World War, and had received awards from several governments. In order to keep themselves entertained in the evening, the cast got up to mischief. Ralph Forbes and Neil Hamilton were involved in pranks of various sorts – capturing live rattlesnakes and keeping them in boxes, outside their tents.

More than their match in the games department, Victor McLaglen would take the snakes out of the boxes, and hide them, leaving the whole team, anxiously looking under their beds and beneath their mattresses, in case, McLaglen had a major surprise in store for them. Mary Brian appeared in the role of Isobel in the film. At this stage Brian was a veteran of a number of Brenon films, so her assessment of him is interesting. "Herbert Brenon was supposedly a very difficult man. I made several pictures with him, and he was always wonderful to me".

In *Beau Geste*, Brenon had a great adventure story, and the movie also offered, the opportunity to present a spectacular landscape on screen. The actor, Ronald Colman impressed Brenon, the lack of ego, the unpretentious professionalism of the man. The British born Colman was a most suave and sophisticated leading man of his generation who ditched the stage, when he proved so popular in silent films. He was also a First World War veteran and had seen serious action. He may have appeared shy and diffident until he went before the cameras, but Colman would transform into this sophisticated, accomplished actor with considerable charisma, while proving excellent at the action scenes, with horses and military equipment. Brenon was buoyed up also by the support of trusted aides, working with him, including J. Roy Hunt, from their earlier collaborations on *War Brides* and *Invasion of Britain*. He could rely too, on first assistant director, Ray Lissner, for support, and the gifted Marie Halvey in the editing department. Every night the rushes (the previous days filming) would be screened to members of Paramount, at a projection room in the

camp, but they elicited no response from the studio executives. Brenon had
to get on with the job of making the film with little studio encouragement,
outside of Jesse Lasky and there were limits here as well. As Brenon
prepared to direct one of the most complex sequences in the movie, the
attack and burning of Fort Zinderneuf, a telegram arrived from Jesse
Lasky. Brenon was accused of exceeding the budget by more than 220,000
dollars. A shocked Brenon was ordered to investigate the situation, Lasky
suggesting that both of their careers were on the line. Brenon needed
another opinion. He contacted his nephew who was a production
accountant. Brenon's nephew took the midnight train from Los Angeles,
and arrived at four in the morning at Yuma, Arizona, where he rested for a
while, in a local hotel. Later that day, he was brought to the camp.
Brenon's nephew identified the overrun as 22,000 not 220,000 dollars.
Brenon was able to wire Lasky about the finances. The show would go on.

In *Beau Geste*, the light and shadow effects, illustrate the expanse of the
desert, creating a dangerous, foreboding atmosphere. In a particularly
memorable scene, Sergeant Le Jaune (Noah Beery) sends two deserters off
in the middle of the endless barren landscape, to die. They beg to be let
stay with the rest of the legion, but Le Jaune, is merciless and refuses.
Brenon seeks to capture an era of bravery and honour, but a gritty, cruel
world as well. A visual spectacle, Brenon created a hypnotic mood and
narrative style – not only through the use of breath-taking images and

action sequences, and the deft characterisation, but also with the film titles, which enhance the atmosphere, and are, in fact, reminiscent of the opening sequence of a later Hollywood movie, *Casablanca*. "Marseilles-Port to that exiled of the self-contained, where lives broken by love – sin – failure – embark for the unquestioning solitude of the Sahara. The canteen, where the legion first becomes a reality to the new recruit, here, among adventurers from every nation, he meets for the first time his comrades of the next five years". The acclaim that Noah Beery received, began to influence the publicity campaign. Advertisements with the emphasis on the character of Sergeant LeJaune began to appear, "monster, savage beast-tamer, pitilessly cruel – and the bravest soldier in the French Foreign Legion. Everyone's talking about Noah Beery's magnificent portrayal of this astounding character, in Herbert Brenon's, *Beau Geste*, a Paramount picture".

The plaudits kept flowing. "Herbert Brenon, who directed this excellent opus, never contributed a better job," the *Motion Picture Classic* would write. "One thing he has accomplished – and that is the quality of the suspense. He shows an assault on the fort that tingles with action and suspense". All the extra work, on script, cast, photography, editing and direction had turned *Beau Geste*, into a personal triumph for Herbert Brenon. "*Beau Geste* takes rank as the first great production of the new picture season", announced the *Los Angeles Times*, quick to recognise the significance of the picture. "It will undoubtedly be seen by everybody, and it will be liked by the great majority because it is a story of valour and mystery as different in plot and theme as any that has ever come".

Beau Geste delivered packed houses. "P.C. Wren's immoderately popular novel of the French Foreign Legion has been turned into a brilliant, colorful and exciting screen melodrama by Herbert Brenon", wrote *Time* magazine in September 1926. "The director has not been afraid to make his romance of three brothers, who loved each other enough to sacrifice life and honor, just a bit brutal, just a little lacking in the usual rose-colors of screen romantics" . In his book, *The Paramount Story*, John Douglas Eames would emphasise that it was "a success rarely exceeded in the whole silent era". After his enormous box office hit, Brenon could take a well-earned rest. He was delighted later to receive the *Photoplay* gold medal, in recognition of the best directed picture of the year and receive feedback from novelist, P.C.Wren. "It is the finest film I have ever seen in my life. It was an astounding thing to me, incredible and awe-inspiring". Brenon's picture helped to define the action film for the next generation. For almost two decades, no Paramount film generated comparable box office receipts. The studio presented Brenon with a diploma, in recognition of his achievement, with *Beau Geste*. When writing in the 1950s, Jesse Lasky acknowledged Paramount's debt of gratitude to the Irish director. "Two of our cinematic landmarks of the twenties were directed by Herbert Brenon – *Peter Pan* and *Beau Geste*. Both pictures have been remade and to my mind fall short of Brenon's inspired prototypes".

Herbert Brenon's name was recognised and carried a cachet for the general public – like D.W. Griffith and Cecil B. De Mille. These names were a draw to cinemagoers in and of themselves, and their identity transcended the public's familiarisation, with any particular film that they had directed. Advertising was beginning to dominate the American landscape and to define America for a new generation. Picking up a magazine in the 1920s, one was as likely to find Brenon advertising Lucky Strike cigarettes, or Lux soap, as to find him talking about a movie. He occupied a world of showbusiness, of American film, of parties and Jazz. He knew many of the richest people in America. He was the quintessential modern man, who walked New York city looking for the great new idea. It was not surprising that a novel like, *The Great Gatsby*, with its contradictory themes and emotions would have interested him. And so it was, that Herbert Brenon became the director of the first film version, of F. Scott Fitzgerald's recently published novel.

"I want a white Rolls-Royce roadster – and I've got to have it by nine o'clock tomorrow morning ", Brenon insisted, to the head of transportation at the studio. The most successful of American film directors was preparing for a movie chronicling the darker side of the American dream. In 1926, only a year after its first publication, Brenon brought *The Great Gatsby* to the screen. Brenon was an inspired choice for this project. He was essentially a critic of modern life in his movies. Scott Fitzgerald's story of a Gotham set of jaded people and the extravagant, yet intensely lonely life, of its central character, was as easy for an East Coast motion picture director to identify with, as tough as it was, to sell to a motion picture public. Brenon made it a prerequisite that his cast read the Fitzgerald novel. The atmosphere that the writer had created, was important for them to absorb. "There was music from my neighbor's house through the summer nights. In his blue gardens men and girls came and went like moths among the whisperings and the champagne and the stars". Warner Baxter was instructed to go and see the Broadway play. Brenon wanted his leading actor to try to imbue himself, as much as possible, with the spirit of Jay Gatsby. Lois Wilson was chosen to play Daisy. The actress was attracted by the challenges and opportunities of the part. "If the Jazz age has done nothing else, its made mothers popular. Only a few years ago, no young actress would play a mother role. It was a sure sign that she was definitely out of the ingénue class. Nightclubs, the Charleston and Prohibition cocktails were taboo. Now all is different. Playing the part of a young mother is merely a tribute to one's versatility. The Jazz mama, similar to Daisy Buchanan which I play in *The Great Gatsby*, is often more attractive than her daughter. So much for the much-decried Jazz Age. Its destructive energies have broken down the line between age and youth".

Although Brenon's work was a film of intrinsic beauty, with impressive interiors, deftly lit by Leo Tover, it also showed men and women rushing up the elaborate staircase in Gatsby's mansion, evidently for sex and many scenes showing the latest in French lingerie. Brenon cast six bathing beauties, enjoying themselves in the pool at one of Gatsby's parties. Brenon in a characteristic comment noted that, "they're the peachiest peaches that ever snuggled into bathing suits". Cinema owners were advised by Paramount, that the book had captivated millions, that the play had run for a year on Broadway, and that the picture was going to be, "the thunderbolt of the season". The film was advertised as "a social satire revealing an unknown side of Gotham's Jazz generation". *New York Times* film critic, Mordaunt Hall summed it up very well. "Gatsby is unknown to most of his guests and some of them are surprised that anyone should want to meet the host. They are a hard lot, satisfied with the entertainment offered to them –modernists who have no gratitude or affection in their souls".

F. Scott Fitzgerald and Herbert Brenon disagreed on some aspects of the adaptation, and the novelist walked out of a screening of the film, unimpressed with the interpretation. Fitzgerald described it as "unspeakably bad", which may have been ironic. It certainly appears to have been unspeakably decadent. Women were shown taking piggyback rides from men, as they cavorted up and down the side of the 'somewhat 'elusive owner's pool. Indeed, Fitzgerald was said to have been disappointed with Warner Baxter, in the central role, who was presented enjoying his own parties a little too much, as if he was playing Herbert Brenon, the movie director, rather than the elusive, shadowy figure from the novel. The movie received much criticism and helped to herald in the era of the strict Hays Censorship Code. The halcyon days of 1916, when Brenon could confidently say, "I never worry about the censors" was gone. *The Great Gatsby* (1926) is one of the lost Brenon films. For the moment, the screenplay, production stills and a short trailer are all that survive.

Leaving Paramount

Herbert credited his wife Helen with the reason he left the stage and vaudeville, to try and make it in the movies. He also attributed to her the idea, all those years ago, that *Ivanhoe* would be a good subject for a film. The couple often holidayed near Lake Saranac, sometimes in Palm Beach, Florida, or on occasion Atlantic City. In New York, they would dine out in the Casino and restaurant in Central Park, among a galaxy of New York's finest, including colleagues from the film industry. Brenon was receiving due acclaim as the famous filmmaker who had made, *The Spanish Dancer, Peter Pan*, and *Beau Geste* — all box office hits for Paramount Pictures. In recognition of Brenon's pioneering role in the film industry, his opinion was frequently sought by journalists, for his views on the future of the American cinema. He always seemed certain of the value of the cinema — both as a source of entertainment, and in advancing America's place in the world. The reputation and status of the country, in his view, was bound up with the images the cinema generated, and which were consumed worldwide.

When not on the set or in the editing room, Brenon liked to go to boxing matches. The film director was a friend and avid supporter of the boxer Jack Dempsey and travelled to his various bouts.

In September 1926, the World Heavyweight contest between the
Champion for many years, the great Jack Dempsey and his opponent Gene
Tunney took place in Philadelphia, at the Sesquicentennial Stadium. It
attracted a packed 130,000 spectators. Among those attending were the
U.S. Vice President, the Secretary of the Treasury, the Secretary of War
and the Secretary of the Navy. The best known names from the film
industry included Charlie Chaplin, Norma Talmadge and Herbert Brenon.
Sadly, it was the end of a terrific boxing career for Dempsey, Tunney
defeating him to become the new World Heavyweight Champion. At
around this juncture, Brenon was based in Park Avenue, New York. The
walls of his upmarket apartment were adorned by memorabilia of the many
celebrities, which were part of his hectic life. Framed letters were
displayed from J.M. Barrie and photographs of people from stage, film and
the sporting world. One picture on the wall was of the boxer Jack
Dempsey, in fighting pose, with an inscription to his friend, Herbert
Brenon.The filmmaker had introduced the boxing champion, to the actress
Estelle Taylor, star of his film, *The Alaskan*. Jack Dempsey and Estelle
Taylor subsequently married. During the 1920s, as the film industry was
beginning to be more active in California, Herbert bought a property in
Malibu. Historically, Malibu was formerly a Spanish Land Grant Mission
called Rancho Topanga, which stretched for twenty one miles along the
California coastline. It was one of the few remaining intact, Spanish
Missions in California, 13,000 acres approximately, and eventually ended
up in the ownership of a wealthy East coast family. However, in the 1920s,
the State began encroaching on part of the land in Malibu and later the

Pacific Coast Highway was constructed. Soon Malibu would become popular with Hollywood's elite. Brenon was one of the first to move in, and be a part of the history of the social world of the West Coast film scene. He had a house at Malibu, and he enjoyed walking along the beach, with his beautiful actress friends or discussing new projects with Jesse Lasky. He would sail his yacht "Brenon's Folly", off the Pacific coast, and organised an annual tennis tournament at his home in Malibu, where his filmmaker friends including Alice Joyce, Anna Q. Nilsson, Ronald Colman and director Roland West, would come and play, or watch the competition unfold, enjoying the beautiful location and atmosphere, as the waves lapped up on the shore beside them.

For Brenon, working on diverse projects was important. He could not make fantasy films all the time, even if they were popular. "A director cannot afford to try for tremendously big pictures every time he picks up his megaphone. I like to make motion picture fantasies like *Peter Pan*, yet I cannot make, with success, more than one of this kind a year". During the winter of 1926, Brenon was in the post-production phases on an adaptation of Dixie Wilsons story, *God Gave Me Twenty Cents*. The story of the disintegrating relationship between a sailor, Steve Doren (Jack Mulhall) and his wife Mary (Lois Moran) was a bittersweet tale, full of the scenes of lowlife, that had also been evident in Brenon's Bowery drama, *The Street of Forgotten Men*. Ma Tapman (Adrienne D'Ambricourt) is the keeper of a Café Dive on the New Orleans waterfront. Brenon recreated the famous New Orleans, Mardi gras, at Paramount's Long Island Studio.

Through extensive use of photographs, an entire New Orleans Street was built. Everything was completed to perfection, from cobbled pavements and flagstones, consistent with Brenon's desire to create the perfect New Orleans atmosphere, while having the ability to control events, in a studio environment. He was taking the editing very seriously. He was trying to avoid titles where possible, while ensuring the key narrative remained intact. He had the usual dodgy characters at the bar, a crowd watching a cockfight, a dancer performing on a table and then Brenon introduces Steve's previous girlfriend Cassie (played by the beautiful Lya de Putti) who, after a brief spell in prison, is seen descending into this hellish place – Brenon intercutting scenes of the club, and its regulars, with Cassie's look of resignation and disgust.

On the evening of November 19, 1926, Paramount Pictures opened its flagship theatre, located in Times Square, New York. The opulent theatre and studio headquarters was the most expensive in America, costing three million dollars to construct. More than a hundred policemen had to control the crowds which gathered outside, to observe the invited guests, at the opening of this imposing new entertainment venue. Searchlights were fixed on the building, which had the effect of drawing more people, which posed some challenges for the New York police department. A significant portion of the west side of Broadway was closed off to pedestrians and disruption caused to parts of Forty-second street. The invited guests, stepped out of limousines, and into the cinema's lobby, which was copiously decorated in marble. Stone tablets, signifying the nations of the world, were to be found off the lobby, in the Hall of Nations. Famed inventor, Thomas Edison, was in the audience, before the film to officially open the Paramount theatre was screened. It was a production by an Irish born filmmaker, Herbert Brenon – one of the greatest directors, of the heyday of the American Cinema. The premiere of *God Gave Me Twenty Cents*, took place to coincide with the opening of the Paramount theatre and office complex on Times Square.

It was also the end of an era. Brenon's days inexplicably were numbered at Paramount. The reception for his film *The Telephone Girl* (1927) was muted. Kitty O' Brien (played by Madge Bellamy) is in charge of a hotel switchboard and gets caught up in a story of shady politics in the New York of the 1920s. Jim Blake is a political boss who attempts to rake up dirt about the past of a political rival. A story of political intrigue, and bribery and how technology could be used to compromise a candidate, it was an interesting theme but made little impact. Bellamy claimed that throughout the filming Brenon was "after her", whatever that meant. To make matters worse, discussions with Jesse Lasky were floundering regarding a new project. The Vice-President of Paramount, believing that Brenon's enthusiasm – indeed the pressure that the film director was exerting on the studio – to support his proposed project *Sorrell and Son*, was a bridge too far. The content of Warwick Deeping's very British novel, was not of obvious appeal to a mainstream cinema audience. The narrative of a soldier who returns from the war, to find that he has been deserted by his wife. He struggles to find employment, but manages to support his young son, through the performance of very menial jobs – a far cry from the conventional heroism, which had resulted in Captain Sorrell, being awarded the military cross. Lasky was adamant that the studio would not back the project in its present form. Upset, Herbert and Helen went on a vacation to Florida. In the press, rumours abounded about what his next move would be. Finally, Herbert announced that he was going to make the film for United Artists – that bastion of artistic freedom – where his friend Joseph Schenck (from his days making films with Norma Talmadge), was now President and Chairman of the Board. He arrived in England on the White Star liner, Olympic on April 2, 1927, to meet the novelist. Together, they visited locations relevant to the story. He had always sought to bring writers on board in the filmmaking process. "I think it is unfair to an author not to work with him as much as possible", he would tell *The Guardian*.

In addition to his leading cast members H.B. Warner and Alice Joyce, Brenon cast a young woman called Mary Nolan, to play the part of the love interest Molly. However, to the public, Mary looked very much like Imogene Wilson. Imogene Wilson was a beautiful blonde Ziegfeld Follie, who as a result of a tempestuous relationship with the vaudeville comedy star Frank Tinney, had become a favourite subject in newspapers across America. This reached its zenith when Tinney punched her, and she ended up with a black eye. The subsequent reaction caused a media furore and the publicity was judged to be too much, even for the boss of the American Follies, who fired Imogene, an action which many felt was a little unfair. In any event, Imogene moved out of New York, tried Hollywood with little success and then left for Europe, where she got some work in Germany. She came back to Hollywood some months later, whereupon Brenon cast her in the United Artists film, *Sorrell and Son*. However, Imogene was credited, as a new actress called Mary Nolan! Hollywood was much amused by Brenon's enthusiasm for the beautiful Imogene, who the director suggested had a great future. In England, he enjoyed, "going about the countryside choosing beautiful scenes for the film, taking my time, my head full of ideas, and the finest human story imaginable, given to me to direct, in the way I feel to be right".

Brenon chose James Wong Howe to photograph *Sorrell and Son*. "My favourite silent director was Herbert Brenon", the cinematographer would later tell historian Kevin Brownlow. "We did many pictures together. He was a fine director. He had great appreciation for artistic camerawork and demanded it ". The team filmed scenes along the River Thames, Westminster Bridge, the Houses of Parliament, and the Savoy, as Captain Sorrell is pictured just back from the war and delighted to see London once again. The euphoria soon turns to despair, as he experiences a series of disappointments – his wife leaves him and he finds that his job has not been kept for him. A modest opportunity at an antique dealership in the town of Staunton comes to nothing. As the Captain falls further into a financial and emotional abyss, the relationship that develops between father and son comes closer, as they struggle to survive, in a grim post war England. Wong Howe recalled the location filming in Britain. "We had beautiful soft light, I remember. There was a little mist and it gave another perspective ".

Eight year old Mickey McBan, (who had also appeared in Brenon's *Peter Pan* film) was chosen for the role of Kit Sorrell. During the English filming of *Sorrell and Son*, a visit was paid to Adelphi Terrace. Sir James Barrie signed two Peter Pan books for the boy, let him sit in his giant fireplace, and showed him a piece of ancient bark with native inscriptions on it, which had previously belonged to Robert Louis Stevenson! As the *Daily Illini* stated, "A father himself, Mr. Brenon believes the story of *Sorrell and Son*, is that of any father and any son, and that the appeal of the film as entertainment is supplemented by its spiritual effect on men and women who view it". In the *Chicago Tribune*, Mae Tinee wrote effusively, "What a tribute and what a reproach is "*Sorrell and Son*"! A tribute to the brave men who fought in the war. A reproach to a civilization that saw them return to a workaday world, jobless and let them stay that way". The *Irish Independent* described it as a "superb picture ". The paper further remarked that, "Mr. Herbert Brenon is the most brilliant and successful man that Dublin has given to the world of films ". Herbert received a best director nomination in the inaugural American Academy Awards. On the 16 June 2005, the American Academy arranged a special screening of *Sorrell and Son*, for the first time since its initial release. The film was part of a new series of Academy screenings headed under the title "Lost and Found". The film had been restored by James Hahn and was screened in

Hollywood. Both the film and screenplay survive, with the latter to be found at the American Academy of Motion Picture Arts and Sciences, another example of the sophisticated attention to detail that Brenon infused all his scripts.

In the late 1920s, Brenon was still demonstrating the energy that had brought him all those earlier movie successes. He had shown creativity, tenacity and sheer determination to see his many projects to successful completion. He managed to be reflective about the demands of individual projects, yet not too reflective about himself. He never second guessed his own suitability for the myriad projects that he took on, and this proved to be a distinct advantage, enabling him to relentlessly march forward, towards new goals and achievements. His attitude to the world was one of optimism and openness, his personal style at this time, a mixture of American film publicity, and Madison Avenue inventiveness, fused with Irish charm and congeniality. He had always been the great ambassador for the American approach, to film production and, indeed, asserting America's claim to dominance in this field. Though this may have grated more than a little bit, on some of the foreign shores he arrived on, he usually found something positive to say about local film production, to prevent himself from being lynched. For all his gifted artistic sensibilities, he was the first group of filmmakers, who were centre stage, as the film industry began outstripping, most other American industries, in economic importance. Britain's *Guardian* newspaper captured the vitality of Brenon in the 1920s. "To meet a director with ideas is always an illuminating experience, but I know of at least half a dozen famous directors in whose company the illumination is lacking in warmth. Herbert Brenon is different; he is simple and friendly, listening just as well as he talks. He sends you away with the feeling that the movies are really not so bad after all, that you yourself are not so bad, and that there are some good films coming. To talk to a man like Brenon is to see the profession of moving pictures in a momentary blaze of understanding".

In his youth, the circus had always captivated Brenon. Now he wanted to do something ambitious on a circus theme, with Lon Chaney. The actor, known as the man of a thousand faces, had gone to Hollywood in 1912, and had an outstanding career, playing character parts, with his capacity to change his appearance, and his expertise at makeup effects, soon causing the industry at large, to hold him in high esteem. *Laugh Clown Laugh*, made in 1928, at the end of the silent era, was a filmed version, of the David Belasco play. It offered Lon Chaney a more complex and thoughtful role, with Brenon in excellent directorial form, and the film boasting a richness in cinematography from James Wong Howe and design from Cedric Gibbons. Lon Chaney was the consummate professional, with an unerring sense of timing and technique. Regardless of what lens was put on the camera, Chaney instantly knew what was required, in terms of the extent of his movement, or gesture. The sheer speed of Chaney, on the logistics of day to day filming, may inadvertently have put newcomer Loretta Young, under even more pressure. Relations between Brenon and the fifteen year old actress in this MGM production were more than frosty. This was her debut role, and he was highly critical of her abilities, which included venting such criticism, in front of the cast and crew, even suggestingin a loud voice, that anyone else would have been better for the role. He found her unresponsive to his directions, and somewhat aloof. At one point, Brenon's unacceptable behaviour stooped to a new low. He threw a chair, at this very new acting talent. At the time, there were many tears and Loretta sought the professional support and comfort of the experienced, Lon Chaney.

In a piece for the *Washington Post*, Brenon outlined some of his methods. "Almost every idea in the human mind is based upon comparison. Almost every human conclusion is based on comparison of one element with another.The surest way, then, to show the nature of a character is to supply another, playing alongside the central one for the audience to compare him with". In *Laugh Clown Laugh* (1928) Brenon was still displaying his great visual flair in this case, recreating European circus visuals, which received favourable comment. The movie nonetheless, was further proof that Brenon had his own filmmaking agenda. His emphasis on complicated social relations, and his willingness to make films which would end on a despairing or ambivalent note, was exemplified in this MGM film, which he made with Irving Thalberg. Nevertheless, *Film Daily*, would comment. "It looks like real money with Lon Chaney in strong sympathetic part. Brenon's clever direction always in evidence". What is remarkable is that Brenon new to this particular studio, and with a penchant for difficult subject material, still managed to make *Laugh Clown Laugh*, MGM's top box office hit for 1928; this was in a year when MGM had film releases from other prominent directors like King Vidor, Erich Von Stroheim, Fred Niblo,Tod Browning and Clarence Brown. He had other causes for celebration as well. A ballot of two hundred critics from across the United States, listed their top ten directors in America for the year 1927/28. Herbert Brenon came out on top, followed by King Vidor, Frank Borzage, Raoul Walsh, Josef Von Sternberg, Victor Fleming, Fred Niblo, Ernest Lubitsch, Charles Chaplin and James Cruze.

Still, Brenon's health had disimproved, marked by increased anxiety and tantrums. He had now developed a problem with alcohol. He was much more alone than before, the uncertainty about future plans was a constant pressure, the project for MGM, was a one off collaboration, and the break with Paramount had been acrimonious. Still, he struggled on. He was a keen sailor, like his brother Chandos, and stories of the ocean had always captured his imagination. He would now select a story that he could bring to the screen, in a compelling manner. For Joseph Conrad and his readers, *The Rescue*, represented a return to characters, which the writer had forsaken, due to the demands of *Lord Jim* and *Heart of Darkness*. Conrad's description of his fictional character, Tom Lingard's fascination with his ship, might also easily apply to Brenon and the cinema.

She represented a run of luck on the Victorian goldfields; his sagacious moderation; long days of planning, of loving care in building; the great joy of his youth, the incomparable freedom of the seas; a perfect because a wandering home; his independence, his love—and his anxiety. He had often heard men say that Tom Lingard cared for nothing on earth but for his brig—and in his thoughts he would smilingly correct the statement by adding that he cared for nothing LIVING but the brig.

Brenon was going to make this dramatic adventure of the sea with producer Sam Goldwyn, who had a preference for movies that could be made for family audiences. The cast starred Ronald Colman, Lily Damita and Alfred Hickman. Colman was cast as Lingard, capturing the essence of the character, bored with life, and compensating by leading an adventurous life on the Java Seas. The film was made on location at Santa Cruz, and photographed by George Barnes. It was a good example of Brenon delivering, when it came to adapting a well-known novel, to the screen. The attractive Lily Damita, played Lady Travers, whose husband is kidnapped by natives, necessitating Lingard's intervention. The location for the demolition of the ship was the Isthmus of Catalina Island. Brenon had twelve motion picture cameras and several still cameras, set up to photograph the scene. The cameras were placed in bomb proof shelters. Up to 140 cases of dynamite were used in the scene. The noise of the blast was heard over thirty miles away. The cost of the brief sequence estimated at fifty thousand dollars.

Key Brenon collaborators on *The Rescue*, included production designer, William Cameron Menzies, film editors Marie Halvey, and Katherine Hilliker and composer Hugo Riesenfeld. Critics were positive about the film which was presented with a synchronised music and effects track, as the sound pictures were beginning to replace the silents.It had been a challenge working with Sam Goldwyn, because he was as fiercely independent and opinionated as the Irish film director. Nonetheless, the tension between producer and director was successful. The *New York Times* was enthusiastic. "Herbert Brenon has done valiant work", it emphasised. " He has skilfully preserved the essence of the narrative…Mr. Brenon sustains the interest throughout his many scenes". At around this time, he was interviewed by the *Hartford Courant*, in an article titled, Director Brenon, Happy Genius. The paper said he was known in the history of Hollywood, as "Battling Brenon, with eyes that can be as blue and smiling as his Killarney skies and then suddenly snap fireworks". *The Rescue* made its way around the world, including to the local seaside Pavilion Cinema, in Brenon's home town of Kingstown, now Dun Laoghaire. It was enjoyed by the residents in the area, where some of the patrons were well aware of Brenon's significance in the film world, and his local heritage. *The Rescue* is preserved at the George Eastman House Museum, in Rochester, New York.

American Talkies

In the beginning, he was hostile to sound on aesthetic grounds. In his opinion, "talkies" had the potential to be a retrograde step – a direct mimicking of the theatrical stage. Furthermore, the silent film form had been built up carefully, over three decades, into a major artistic and financial endeavour, so in his view, any new departure carried substantial economic, as well as artistic risks. "The full length talking film play – will have to omit or slight the very things that differentiate the art of the motion picture from that of the stage ", he argued in 1928, as he outlined his aesthetic concerns. "These things are the sweep of its canvas, its scenic beauty, its suggestive images, and the finesse of its action or interpretive movement, all its significant photographic detail". This initial, somewhat trenchant assessment, led to an argument sometimes put forward that the talkative, garrulous, Irishman, was somehow, inexplicably, unsuited to sound, made one or two talkies, and subsequently faded from view. The reality is altogether different. Nonetheless, forever the showman, Brenon announced, "I don't believe the silent picture will ever die", as he proceeded to direct his first talking picture in 1929.

Lummox was based on a popular novel of the time, by the Ohio born novelist Fannie Hurst, who had a following and reputation, for her literary portrayals of somewhat, realistic women characters, in fiction. Her best known novels included, *Stardust: The Story of An American Girl, Lummox,* and *A President is Born*, *Back Street* and *Imitation of Life*. She was also an important figure in sexual politics in America, during the first half of the 20th century, both in her fiction, and presenting radio shows, where hitherto taboo sexual topics – in particular homosexuality – began to be more openly discussed. In *Lummox*, a servant girl, gets romantically involved with the son of her employer. She discovers that she is pregnant, but that he is engaged to a rich society girl. The girl leaves her employment, gives the baby up for adoption, and then watches him grow up, in the household of another wealthy family, and become a noted, concert pianist. It was intriguing that the story of a troubled, inarticulate woman, should have been Brenon's choice for his first sound film. Elizabeth Meehan adapted the novel, spending several weeks, working with Hurst in New York, and Brenon joined them for the preparation of the final draft.

The film director was sophisticated and convivial, generating an enjoyable creative atmosphere in the pre-production phases of projects. Hurst remembered him fondly, and at how different he was to the typical west coast filmmakers, who tended to ignore the views of writers and novelists. "I liked Brenon greatly – he was my favourite of the picture people. He was a poetic Irishman- very funny and warm. I went to the Coast for one of my pictures and they totally ignored me – so I went home after five weeks. I never really adjusted to life out there. It was a vacuum. They lived a life completely enclosed. Their circle was a dime. They talked nothing but motion pictures. Everything else went out the window. Some fine authors went out there and were sucked into the vacuum and lost forever".

The actress chosen to play the lead was a relative newcomer; indeed, if she was known at all, it was for being married to the actor, William S. Hart. "The girl who wanted to do this waited in the lobby of the hotel with a picture of herself in the part. Her name was Winifred Westover. She was the most persistent person I ever met in my life", Hurst, ruefully remembered. "Herbert Brenon and I were searching everywhere for the star who would be right for Lummox, but we had to give up and we had to use Westover. It was a pity because this was my favourite story".

Dealing with love scenes in talking pictures, was going to be challenging, without Brenon's accustomed underscoring of the scene with his troupe of musicians. Neither could he, verbally encourage his actors along, while the scene was being recorded. Brenon summed up the new situation. "I wouldn't go so far as to say two people must actually be in love when their affections are being recorded, but they must feel they are in love at the moment. The days of the silent love scene, when the sweethearts were in the so-called 'clutch', with one of them thinking about what she was going to have for dinner and the other worrying about his Income tax are over". The distinguished German cinematographer Karl Struss (who had collaborated with F.W. Murnau on Sunrise) photographed the picture. The director of *Lummox*, was not always easy to deal with. Indeed, some would claim that the former silent director still acted like a colonial tyrant, showing little sensitivity towards his crew members or cast, even in the more collaborative studio dominated sound era of the 1930s. Brenon had clear views about the new element of sound. "I do not believe in the introduction of outside or background sounds unless it distinctly performs some psychological duty. For example to secure realism in sound production, some directors have incorporated the ticking of a clock. While this was at first a novelty, it has long ago ceased to be that, and has become only a distracting nuisance". Some impressive set designs by William Cameron Menzies (later production designer on *Gone With the Wind*) could not disguise a tentativeness with the production in general. Though thematically ambitious, it was not well received. Nonetheless, it was a further indication of Brenon's interest in realism in the cinema, which he combined throughout his career, inexplicably, with a taste for fantasy and the sentimental 'Brenon touch' often referred to by critics. The lukewarm response to *Lummox*, even the *Daily Express* found it "gloomy", and the wider realisation that the talkies were here to stay, had begun to depress him by 1930. "I am heavy-hearted about the effect the talkies have had on the silent pictures. I have watched the growth and development of the silent films through so many years, worked and planned for their progress. They had reached a point when they were almost perfect, and suddenly – the whole status of the film industry changed. It was like a pack of cards falling down". He was buoyed up when he heard that President Hoover had viewed some talkies, but had found that there was, in essence, " too much going on" in them, for his liking. Brenon envisaged a day when silent films and talkies would be screened in different cinemas side by side, catering for different tastes.

After the turf war, between the East and West coast operations of Paramount, William Le Baron had been forced out, and took up an executive position, at the newly formed RKO. It was reasonable to assume that RKO would also be an encouraging home for Brenon. He made a move to the studio to make, *The Case of Sergeant Grischa* (1930). If any more proof was needed, Brenon was displaying his attraction to challenging subject matter, taking on the first film version, of a harrowing German war novel. "My most difficult problem is to find the right man for Grischa. No mere matinee idol will do", Brenon told reporters. "The boy who plays this lead must have the profoundest understanding of dramatic values. He must live the part. He must visualise in his person the helplessness, the hopelessness, and the resignation of the individual who went to battle at the command of gold lace and military pomp, the pawn of Emperor and King, the sacrifice to the Moloch of war ". Brenon cast Chester Morris to play Sergeant Grischa. Betty Compson, Alec B. Francis and Jean Hersholt rounded out the cast. The presence of the very pretty Betty Compson, for this grim tale, appeared incongruous. Nonetheless, she was a popular American actress of the time, and this was an RKO picture. In choosing Betty Compson, (who had appeared in his first Paramount film, *The Rustle of Silk*) Brenon was also displaying his American film industry roots. A director not averse to taking on difficult subject matter, but one who nevertheless, built the American industry around stars, and public identification with stars.

The movie featured many war veterans, in key roles, and a former major in the German army, acted as the military consultant. The commercial possibilities for this RKO production, cannot have been helped, by Brenon's prescriptiveness. He was adamant that this was to be like no other war film. There were to be no battle scenes, and only one gunshot fired, and even that was to occur, only at the end of the film. "Sergeant Grischa is one of those things that somehow get in and come out of a class A studio, despite its story, and then is called a fine production, without commercial possibilities or mass appeal ", the *Variety* reviewer picking up, on some of Brenon's predilections: " In the picture business the presumption is that entertainment sells. As a business the first thought is, or should be, of the box office". The public reaction to the film was mixed. One critic remarking that when the war got particularly desperate, Betty simply looked like a tough girl camping out in the forest. The rest of the time, most of her American makeup was left largely intact. However, *Photoplay* described it as a "compelling drama marching relentlessly to a tragic close".

In *The Great Gatsby*, *Laugh Clown Laugh*, and *The Case of Sergeant Grischa*, to take just three examples, the chief protagonist dies, before the end of the film. This tendency was certainly not a helpful factor for Brenon, if he wished to remain within the Hollywood system. A realist tendency can be identified, within Brenon's films, across almost all the various genres. He is unafraid to thwart the satisfaction of his audience, as he attempts to stretch the boundaries of what is possible in the commercial cinema. While some of the reviews for *The Case of Sergeant Grischa*, were disappointing for Brenon, he was still not without fans, in America. In 1930, in a poll of two hundred American critics, he was still ranked in the top ten film directors for that year. Only Cecil B. De Mille could claim such success and high profile longevity in the industry, and arguably with a much narrower range of subject material. In 1930, Brenon made a trip to Dublin, and was interviewed by the *Sunday Independent*, in the Shelbourne hotel, where he spoke about his intention of making a film in Ireland. "As sure as I am sitting in this chair I will do a picture here. The principal thing is the story. It is useless to do a film which will appeal to the Irish people only". On visits to Ireland, he often stayed with his friend, the celebrated tenor, Count John McCormack, at Moore Abbey.

Back in the United States, Brenon was finding his American talkies challenging, in terms of meeting box office expectations. It was time to return to safer ground, to characters and subject matter that had helped to establish his reputation. *Film Daily* announced that he had completed casting for *Beau Ideal*, in September, 1930. Brenon was returning to the desert, in search of inspiration. He proved to be in excellent form again, with a series of impressive action set pieces, and was re-united with his friend, Texan cinematographer, J. Roy Hunt. Together, they captured stunning, dramatic images, of foreign legion troops, trekking across, inhospitable, landscapes. Ralph Forbes returned from the earlier film, reprising his role of the only surviving brother, John Geste. In the movie Loretta Young plays Isobel – the woman loved by both John Geste and Otis Madison. It is a sweet and effective performance. Loretta Young clearly better able to handle Brenon on this occasion. The Judge Advocate (played by John M. St Polis with significant presence) presides over the fate of a court marshalled John Geste, who at his persuasion, gets Geste's inevitable death sentence, commuted to ten years penal servitude. It is a pretty harrowing prospect, but as the Judge informs Geste, "it could have been worse, much worse my boy", as John Geste is taken away, to scenes of a weeping Isobel.

In *Beau Ideal*, the arabs look benign initially, but prove, untrustworthy, no doubt the imposition of an unfair western stereotype. But Brenon can be remarkably, even handed, in his presentation of the characters. The legion attracts, a most desperate group, and the Geste's are as likely to make meaningful alliances, with people of other faiths. In *Beau Ideal* there are some outstanding shots and compositions, which show the Brenon, feel for drama, atmosphere and editing technique. However, the image of the Gestes as an extraordinary English family, albeit with some issues, has diminished. The film is portrayed more tongue in cheek, than was evident in the first film. After all, the last remaining of the heroic English brothers is now wholly dependent, on an American to be rescued. *Beau Ideal* is an early American talking picture. What is striking is that it is more visual and fluid than one would have expected for such an early sound film. Brenon, who brought audiences *Ivanhoe*, *Peter Pan* and *The Spanish Dancer*, takes a further significant step, with both the silent *Beau Geste*, and its sound sequel and appears to be setting the outline of what one might consider the parameters of the Classical, Hollywood Cinema. Ralph Forbes featured on the front cover of the March 1931, edition of *American Cinematographer* magazine, in a suitably impressive rugged outdoor shot, which helped to promote the film among industry watchers.

Brenon's stint at RKO was proving worthwhile. He retained control over his projects, and was able to deal with themes which appealed to him. Ebullient, in person, Brenon's modernity, ironically, called into question, the optimism of American society. In *Transgression*, America's sophisticated and grown up filmmaker, was back to his other world of interiors and psychology and adultery – and the secrets that people keep from one another – as he teamed up with actress Kay Francis and Ricardo Cortez, for an adaptation of Kate Jordan's novel of the same name. *New York Times* considered that for the most part it was, "an intelligently filmed story" and that there are "some compelling atmospheric effects in some of the sequences".

The Mexican actress, Dolores Del Rio, had developed a following in the silent cinema, appearing in some films directed by Raoul Walsh. She was one of the most beautiful women that ever graced the silver screen, and now Brenon was helping her make the transition to talkies, with a role where her strong accent, and shaky English, would not be out of place. In *Girl of the Rio* (1932) she plays a beautiful cafe singer, known as the Dove. Don Jose Maria Lopez (Leo Carillo) is trying to make advances, and given that he is a millionaire, lives on a huge hacienda, and considers himself to be the "best caballero in all Mexico", is not happy when the cafe singer rejects him, in favour of a young gambler. Del Rio represented the exotic in the Hollywood cinema and film directors played this up. She became a major star and also a Hollywood celebrity couple, when she married MGM's Head of Design, Cedric Gibbons. Through her cinematic achievements, she would later become an important role model to young actresses, particularly in Latin America. However, as one might expect with Brenon, controversy was never far away. In the United States, in May 1932, a storm of protest erupted over the film. Mexico was said to be angry, over the manner in which the country had been depicted. There was a furious response from politicians who considered the film to be highly insulting to the country, a situation made worse, by the fact that the leading cast, Dolores Del Rio, and Leo Carillo were Mexicans. The Mexican Revolutionary party, threatened to storm a cinema. The Mexican Embassy in Washington, lodged a protest. The Republic of Panama, banned the film and the Governor of Chiapas, refused permission, for it to be screened in Chiapas. Brenon must have been glad to get away from the United States, at this time. He treated himself to a European vacation, and in England purchased a farm in a quiet village called Elstead, in Surrey. In July 1932, he was in Ireland meeting relations, including his Uncle George of the Dublin United Tramway company. In Dublin, he visited the headquarters of the Independent newspaper group in the company of Walter McNally, of Radio Pictures (RKO). The Journalist that they were due to meet, had gone off to Leinster House, the seat of the Irish parliament. So Brenon and Walter headed off in the same direction whereupon, on arrival, Brenon, revelling at being in Leinster House, for the first time, expressed a desire in the future, to make a film, set in the Irish parliament! The Irish nationalist tendencies of the Brenon family had been amply demonstrated since the 1880s. *Shamus O' Brien* and *Kathleen Mavourneen* were examples of Herbert's own Irish themed films. Brenon was in great form, happier than he had been in years, even if official Ireland had not received his films too kindly.

In 1923, the Irish State had appointed James Montgomery as the first film censor and in this role, he had enthusiastically made cuts to *Beau Geste*, and banned Brenon's jazz age films, *The Great Gatsby*, and *Dancing Mothers*, in Ireland. In what must undoubtedly, have been quite an experience for both men, the film director visited the film censor, in his Dublin office. Brenon was expecting to meet someone reflecting, as he put it, "the manners of a Marquis, with the morals of a Methodist". If so, he was caught completely off-guard. He found the Irish censor, a friend of poet W.B. Yeats, to be a brilliant, witty, conversationalist – very likely to have been comfortable in the environment of the sophisticated salons, which Herbert's mother Frances had held many years before – where Parnell, Oscar Wilde and other notable figures attended.

Brenon returned to America with a new perspective on a range of issues. In the United States, Walter Wanger wanted Brenon to direct, *The Bitter Tea of General Yen*, but the director wanted out of his profit sharing RKO contract and the film was offered to, a more unlikely, Frank Capra and eventually made for Columbia. The newspapers and magazines at this time were full of stories regarding a tussle for the film rights of Charles Dickens novel, *Oliver Twist*. The small American studio, Monogram won out and the British film executive I.E Chadwick became the Executive Producer of a 1933 version of the film. Brenon was initially scheduled to direct, but arguments over money caused him to withdraw. Instead he agreed to act as supervisor of the film, with William Cowen directing. However, it is interesting to note that Brenon put much of the team together for this film.

Elizabeth Meehan undertaking the adaptation, Carl Pierson who had cut a number of Brenon projects was the film editor, and the talented child actor, Dickie Moore, who had appeared in Brenon's film, *Sorrell and Son*, was selected to play Oliver.The picture opened in New York, in April 1933.

Elstree

His American talkies, had been interesting, unusual, but not particularly successful, and although Herbert Brenon would always be considered one of the great pioneering figures of the American cinema – that industry was changing. For most of his silent career Brenon called the shots and he was either too old, or to intransigent to change his approach, now that the talkies were all the rage. The new producers and executives on the block were different and included Lewis Selznick's son, David O. Selznick, (now controlling production at RKO). They expected to share, at least some of the control with directors. Nonetheless, the Irishman having articulated the industrial fact of American film, as early as 1915 – "it is an industry, but we do our best to make it an art" – was far from downhearted. He was pragmatic enough, not to expect an industry to be grateful, or sentimental. He had vision and aesthetic talents, but also resilience. Now aged fifty five, he would make the move that was best for him. He would go to England, live on a farm, and spend the next five years, at Elstree, making films in his own, inimitable way, and at his own pace. Through the leadership of John Maxwell and via British International Pictures (B.I.P.) an obscure area of England, now named Elstree, had been turned into a centre of film production, attracting key indigenous and international talent. In 1935, Herbert Brenon signed a contract with British International Pictures, to make films in England.

His first major project at Elstree was *Living Dangerously* (1936). The talented Otto Kruger plays Dr. Norton, a famous specialist, who has to face the General Medical Council, and answer a charge of unprofessional conduct, brought against him by his partner. The charge is false, but the circumstantial evidence is so overwhelming that his name is erased from the medical register! The story switches to the United States. An impressive set, featuring a New York Penthouse, the home of Dr. Norton was built at Elstree, with skyscrapers, visible in the background. The set was true Americana, from the cocktail bar and ultra-modern furniture and fittings, which surprised some of the British working on the film, at Elstree, in the 1930s. The art director was Cedric Dawe and the cinematographer Bryan Langley. The film was well received with Britain's *Observer* newspaper impressed with Otto Kruger's performance. "He is one of the more sensitive and intellectual of America's screen actors; he knows all the physical tricks of acting, and he has a flair for the emotional ones. Above all, he has irony, which is far rarer in the cinema than wit".

Brenon's home during the Elstree years, was a farm in Surrey, which he had bought some years before. His notepaper at this time was humorous. It read at the top of the page in the centre, and in a gothic typescript, reminiscent of the era of Ivanhoe, – the Home Farm, Hookley Lane, Surrey. On the right hand side of the page was typed, New Laid Eggs and Table Poultry. The British telephone directory, listed him as a poultry farmer. In Britain, on paper, at any rate, he was a farmer, as well as a filmmaker. He took much delight in this contrast. In the 1930s, Brenon was expressing himself off-screen as well. In London, he could be found dining at Claridges, the Savoy, or at the Ritz. British newspapers and magazines were ready to quote him, every bit as enthusiastically and frequently as their American cousins. At Elstree, he was a film director moving from Hollywood to Britain in the 1930s, rather than the more usual reverse scenario. This makes the films interesting to study in terms of certain cultural and stylistic tensions, and choice of subject matter and visual treatment. His collaborators are also not infrequently, Europeans in exile in Britain, which gives something of the flavour of Elstree at the time.

The Dominant Sex (1937) was about the challenges of domestic life, and the right of women to fair treatment in marriage. The director enjoyed the performances and feisty dialogue delivered by the young British actress Diana Churchill, making her first major film debut, opposite Philips Holmes. Churchill played the outspoken woman, arguing with her husband about equality – insisting on a stronger say, in how they should live their lives, as husband and wife. The film represents the modernity of Herbert Brenon and demonstrates the impact of his life in America, and how this could be brought to bear on the subjects, he chose to direct in England, in the 1930s. The critical response to the film was mixed. Some publications arguing, that the idea that a woman should have individuality, or an expectation of this, after marriage, to be an unusual subject for a film.

Brenon was, in essence by now, a true New York libertarian, somewhat comically, anachronistic for his time, in rural England, when out of the company of the props and buildings and intellectual exchanges, of the great American metropolis. Still, *The Dominant Sex* should have been no surprise, to anyone familiar with the maker of the 1920s jazz age film, *Dancing Mothers*, and there was some positive British press reaction. "Every husband and wife, whether they be young or old, will recognise something of themselves in *The Dominant Sex*. Every woman will sympathise with, Miss Diana Churchill, as the young wife who approaches her married life intending to keep the independence of single days, but who, as a result, finds herself in perpetual conflict with her husband. *The Dominant Sex* is an outstanding British film- It is brisk and cleverly acted, is intimate, and has a real human theme". The film was screened in London, at the New Gallery cinema, on Regent Street, where it was promoted as a "daringly intimate comedy drama of young married couples striving for self-expression".

A movie version of Ian Hays bestselling novel and play, *Housemaster* was next on Brenon's agenda. The narrative concerned the interaction of three girls in an all boy's school. Brenon, with his privileged English private education, at Colet Court / St. Pauls and at Kings College London, was able to capture the insularity and claustrophobic quality, of an English public school, very authentically. The director displayed his talent at generating mood, in interior sequences that are memorable, leading Producer Walter Mycroft to state that the "emotional Irishman was inspired to something like the *Beau Geste* form, which had made him famous". The critic from the *Observer* newspaper was also enthusiastic. "The *Housemaster* is good hearty fun all along the line, but Otto Kruger's performance in the name-part makes it something better. For some reason not clearly apparent, Mr. Kruger seems to believe in this preposterous school, and feel real concern over the well-being of these incredible youngsters... As an American, he was shy, I am told, of taking up a part so typically and traditionally English. He need not have worried. His housemaster has something better than the stamp of Eton and Harrow".

If Herbert Brenon had a deft touch, dealing with comic episodes, he tended to avoid comedies in his career. Nevertheless, he had a notable success with a popular play, by Eden and Adelaide Philpotts. *Yellow Sands* (1938) has to be considered one of Brenon's finest films, he was totally in sympathy with his subject, and let his talent for exterior filming, and the power of landscape, free rein. The newspapers were excited about the production from the outset. "All Devon and Cornwall have been searched for a place to make this film, and nowhere is there a fishing village that so nearly matches the one described by the author as Sennan Cove". The distinguished British actress, Dame Marie Tempest, took on the role of Jennifer Harwell – a wealthy woman, whose will surprises and angers those left behind – when she chooses a nephew with extreme left wing beliefs, as the sole recipient of her estate. In 1938, Herbert was still attracting high levels of press attention. "Hundreds of people have been journeying to St. Levan Church during the past week, to watch Mr. Herbert Brenon the famous Irish film producer, directing the making of "Yellow Sands", the *Cornishman* newspaper would write.

The reception for the film was positive. The Times of London noting, "The cool, fresh winds from the lovely western countryside seem to have blown away the cobwebs of the studio, and the quiet dignity of fields and sea provides the atmosphere which each player has so well absorbed".

Brenon's work in the sound era, can be summarised as being confined largely to low key melodramas. He was still showing his interest in domestic dramas and unusual family situations. In *Black Eyes* (1939) we have another father/daughter relationship. Ivan Petroff (Otto Kruger) works as a head waiter in an exclusive establishment in Moscow, but his daughter Tanya (Mary Maguire) who lives with him in a large house, assumes that he is in business. The daughter rarely goes out, as her father is very protective, and her life is still organised by her governess, although she is now a young adult. She has regular music lessons with a man, who is beginning to show some romantic interest. The father appears to tolerate this, but Brenon's presentation of the Otto Kruger character, makes it appear, as though the father is a rival for her affections, and there is some ambiguity, as to the exact nature of their relationship. Ivan gets involved in a financial deal with a businessman who develops a fondness for his daughter. At a rendezvous at the restaurant, the waiter's daughter discovers what her father does for a living. She accuses him of deceiving her, and keeping her locked up at home.

The deal between her father and the businessman falls through, leaving his ambitions of improving his position, and thereby, impressing his daughter, dashed. This is typical of the Brenon material in the sound era. The subjects are very trivial on the surface, but there are undercurrents. Human vices are frequently presented and the fallibility of his characters comes across, in a striking way, in contrast to the heroic protagonists of Hollywood. His last film, *The Flying Squad* (1940) an adaptation of Edgar Wallace's police novel, starring Sebastian Shaw was not his finest talkie, but Brenon could be proud of his Elstree achievements, a record of accomplishment and an extension, in some cases of thematic ideas, explored during his American career. In 1940, activities stopped at Elstree and the British army moved in, to requisition the facilities. At this troubled time, Herbert Brenon, had more options than most, and returned to the United States, and the more comfortable environment, of the West Coast.

Home was now the attractive and sedate, La Mirada Avenue, in California, where the population was less than three hundred, and where orange, lemon and grapefruit trees dominated the landscape. For a few years, Brenon toyed with the idea of making some more films, but the intensity of his earlier life, had finally caught up with him. "I was 63. I was nearing a complete nervous breakdown. Also, I realised that I had passed my peak. There was nothing left for me but to direct less important pictures. I didn't want that. One of the things that depresses me about Hollywood is to visit sets and see once famous faces now doing bit parts or extra roles. I decided to quit".

He believed that many of the films made in the 1940s and 1950s, were being manufactured on an assembly line basis. They lacked in his view, "the individuality that directors of the past, were allowed to inject". In California, he was still in regular contact with many of his former colleagues including, the younger generation of Americans, whose careers he had launched. James Wong Howe and Mary Brian would call by, and they would have a great time, remembering their adventures together, making pictures. The theatrical actress and television star, Mary Martin would seek his advice and he kept in touch with Sam Fuller, who had worked as an assistant director for him, before embarking on a successful film directing career of his own. Fuller looked to Brenon as a great mentor and father figure. In January 1950, Brenon was celebrating his 70th birthday. It was mostly a private affair with Helen and the family, but his birthday had given him a new lease of life. He was now looking at a mystery story which had been written by Rupert Hughes. Brenon owned the rights and was planning to bring the story to the screen. During this point, the film historian, George Geltzer contacted Brenon with a view to penning an article about his work, for the magazine, *Films in Review*. On March 13, 1955, Brenon wrote, "Thank you so much for the copies of *Films in Review*. It is splendidly done".

He was enjoying the comfortable California life with Helen, devoted wife from their vaudeville days, all those decades ago. There was plenty to do and see, and almost all the people he knew from his cinema days were now based in California. His son Cyril would help out when needed, and he had his nieces and nephews constantly visiting, so he was not lonely. When

Gladwin Hill of the *Los Angeles Times*, interviewed Brenon in Hollywood in the 1950s, she found a 73 year old man, happy with his lot in life. Still married to Helen Oberg, he had made sensible real estate investments, in Malibu, and elsewhere. He was not making films, but was collecting rents. He observed the current Hollywood film scene with interest, and with no regrets. Happy to be a dapper guest at the recent premiere of the Disney animated version of *Peter Pan*, which he enjoyed, even if he felt, it was more Disney, than Barrie.

On June 21, 1958, Herbert Brenon died in Los Angeles, after some struggles with a heart condition. He was 78 years old. In her famous Hollywood film column, Louella Parsons would write that "Herbert Brenon, who died Saturday, was one of the greats of his time". In its obituary, the Times of London noted that he was: "A leading director in the early days of the cinema, and many of the best known and still remembered film plays of the days before "talkies" were his work, such as *Peter Pan*, *Beau Geste* and an early version of *Ivanhoe*. He sought to raise standards with screenplays which had real artistic merit. He was one of the first to make longer films". The obituaries in the *Los Angeles Times* and the *New York Times* summed it up most succinctly, emphasising that Herbert Brenon was one of the "big three" of the heyday of the American cinema. His remains were brought to New York, to be buried. The location, perhaps, the most beautiful cemetery in the world, the 400 acres of rolling hills that make up Woodlawn Cemetery, in the Bronx. Here he would be laid to rest in this most historic of places, that contains so many of America's most famous artists, politicians and businessmen, from Irving

Berlin, who provided a song for *The Passion Flower*, or George M. Cohan the subject of Brenon's film, *The Song and Dance Man*. Herbert Brenon's final resting place was spectacular, in more ways than one. No mean grave, rather a mausoleum of some scale, with an entrance and outside, the Brenon name, writ large enough to be legible at some distance, from the monument. The structure itself had a castellated roof, making it look like a miniature castle, which had stepped out of the production of *Ivanhoe*. Unusually, a clock finished off the elaborate design. Touchstone was still alive and well.

Following his death, Herbert Brenon films began to be screened at a number of venues, primarily at the George Eastman House Museum, where the curator James Card, had a particular devotion to the *Peter Pan* film and was responsible for its restoration. In New York, at the Theodore Huff Memorial Film Society, William K. Everson (later Professor of Film Studies, at New York University) would screen films from the silent era. Brenon films would often be among the most popular of screenings. The work of Herbert Brenon was featured in Kevin Brownlow's *Hollywood* television series, while historian, Jack Lodge, made an important contribution to Brenon studies with his writings on the filmmaker, for the publication *Griffithania*. In Italy, the Pordenone Silent film festival celebrated Brenon's work. Today many of Brenon's films are to be found in private collections and at research institutes throughout the world. *Ivanhoe* at the national film archive, in Britain. *Peter Pan* and *The Rescue*, at the George Eastman House museum, Rochester, New York.

In California, the UCLA film archive holds copies of *Beau Geste*, *Beau Ideal* and *Dancing Mothers*. *The Spanish Dancer* was recently restored by the Dutch Film Institute EYE, in Amsterdam. *A Kiss for Cinderella* is to be found at the Museum of Modern Art, New York. In Washington, the Library of Congress, holds a copy of *The Street of Forgotten Men*, and copies of the films Brenon made, with Norma Talmadge. Many of his British talkies are to be found at the national film archive, including *Housemaster*, *Yellow Sands* and *Black Eyes*. Herbert Brenon's vision of a world where silent films would continue to be shown, has come about. Silent film festivals are gaining in popularity and the industry is respecting the achievements of the great filmmakers of the past. Turner Classic Movies, Warner Brothers, MGM and Miramax films among others, have made the era of these artists of interest to the public again, by releasing their films or supporting new artistic works, which vividly bring that world to life again, for younger audiences.

Herbert Brenon's life had encapsulated so wonderfully, a sense of excitement and urgency. He was at the centre of everything, collaborating with the major stars and writers of the day, identifying talent in design, music and cinematography which would continue to impact for decades in the cinema. He was one of the first to argue for film to be part of the American academic curriculum. Herbert Brenon had not invented the cinema, but he had been responsible, in so many ways, for the manner in which it had developed, to become the great art form of the 20th century.

Select Filmography

All for Her (1912)

The Clown's Triumph (1912)

Camille (1912)

The Dividing Line (1912)

The Blind Musician (1912)

The Fugitives (1912)

Leah, the Forsaken (1912)

Vengeance (1912)

No Greater Love (1912)

Lass O' the Light (1912)

The Long Strike (1912)

The New Magdalen (1912)

Rags and Riches (1913)

In a Woman's Power (1913)

Dr. Jekyll and Mr. Hyde (1913)

Kathleen Mavourneen (1913)

The Bishop's Candlesticks (1913)

Blood Will Tell (1913)

She Never Knew (1913)

Secret Service Sam (1913)

The Angel of Death (1913)

The Last of the Madisons (1913)

Robespierre (1913)

Across the Atlantic (1913)

Ivanhoe (1913)

Mr and Mrs Innocence Abroad (1913)

The Anarchist (1913)

Lost in the Streets of Paris (1913)

Absinthe (1913)

Time is Money (1913)

Love or a Throne (1913)

Love and a Lottery Ticket (1913)

Watchdog of the Deep (1914)

The Price of Sacrilege (1914)

An Old Rag Doll (1914)

Neptune's Daughter (1914)

When the World Was Silent (1914)

When the Heart Calls (1914)

Redemption (1914)

The Tenth Commandment (1914)

In Self Defense (1914)

Peg O' the Wilds (1914)

Life's Shop Window (1914)

She Was His Mother (1915)

The Awaited Hour (1915)

The Heart of Maryland (1915)

The Kreutzer Sonata (1915)

The Clemenceau Case (1915)

The Two Orphans (1915)

Sin (1915)

The Soul of Broadway (1915)

A Daughter of the Gods (1916)

War Brides (1916)

The Eternal Sin (1917)

The Lone Wolf (1917)

The Fall of the Romanoffs (1917)

Empty Pockets (1918)

The Passing of the Third Floor Back (1918)

The Invasion of Britain (1918)

Twelve Ten (1919)

The Mysterious Princess (1920)

Sister Against Sister (1920)

Beatrice (1920)

The Passion Flower (1921)

The Sign on the Door (1921)

The Wonderful Thing (1921)

Any Wife (1922)

A Stage Romance (1922)

Shackles of Gold (1922)

Moonshine Valley (1922)

The Custard Cup (1923)

The Rustle of Silk (1923)

The Woman with Four Faces (1923)

The Spanish Dancer (1923)

Shadows of Paris (1924)

The Breaking Point (1924)

The Side Show of Life (1924)

The Alaskan (1924)

Peter Pan (1924)

The Little French Girl (1925)

The Street of Forgotten Men (1925)

A Kiss for Cinderella (1925)

The Song and Dance Man (1926)

Dancing Mothers (1926)

Beau Geste (1926)

The Great Gatsby (1926)

God Gave Me Twenty Cents (1926)

The Telephone Girl (1927)

Sorrell and Son (1927)

Laugh Clown Laugh (1928)

The Rescue (1929)

Lummox (1930)

The Case of Sergeant Grischa (1930)

Beau Ideal (1931)

Transgression (1931)

Girl of the Rio (1932)

Wine, Women and Song (1933)

Royal Cavalcade (1935)

Honors Easy (1935)

Living Dangerously (1936)

Someone at the Door (1936)

The Dominant Sex (1937)

Spring Handicap (1937)

The Live Wire (1937)

Housemaster (1938)

Yellow Sands (1938)

Black Eyes (1939)

The Flying Squad (1940)

Select Bibliography

Bernstein, Matthew (1994) *Walter Wanger: Hollywood Independent*, University of California Press.

Bordwell, David, Janet Staiger and Kristin Thompson (1985) *The Classical Hollywood Cinema: Film Style and Mode of Production to 1960*, London, Routledge

Brownlow, Kevin (1968) *The Parade's Gone By*, University of California Press

Brownlow, Kevin (1976) *The War, The West and The Wilderness*, New York, Knopf

Conrad, Joseph (1920) *The Rescue*, J.M. Dent

Cook, Pam (1992) *The Cinema Book*, London, British Film Institute

Dick, Bernard (2011) *Hollywood Madonna*, University Press of Missisippi

Dumaux, Sally (2002) *King Baggot*, North Carolina, McFarland & Company

Eames, John Douglas (1985) *The Paramount Story*, Octopus Press

Elsaesser Thomas (1990) *Early Cinema: Space Frame Narrative*, London, BFI

Everson, William (1998) *American Silent Cinema*, Da Capo Press

Fairbanks Jr, Douglas (1988) *The Salad Days*, New York, Doubleday

Fitzgerald, F. Scott (1925) *The Great Gatsby*, Charles Scribner's Sons, New York

Gibson, Emily and Barbara Firth (2005) *The Original Million Dollar Mermaid*, Allen and Unwin

Geltzer, George (1955) Hebert Brenon, Films in Review

Golden, Eve (1996) *Vamp, the Rise and Fall of Theda Bara*, New York, Emprise Publishing

Hansen, Miriam (1994) *Babel and Babylon: Spectatorship in American Silent Film*, Harvard University Press

Koszarski, Richard (2010) *Hollywood on the Hudson*, Rutgers University Press

Lasky, Jesse (1957) *I Blow My Own Horn*, New York, Doubleday

Lodge, Jack (1996) *The Career of Herbert Brenon*, Griffithania

Low, Rachael (1950) *The History of the British Film 1914-1918*, London, George Allen & Unwin

Mycroft, Walter (2006) *The Memoirs of a British Film Producer*, Scarecrow Press

Neale, Stephen (1981) *Genre*. London, BFI

Schatz, Thomas (1998) *The Genius of the System.Hollywood Film-making in the Studio Era*. London, Faber and Faber.

Slide, Anthony (2002) *Silent Players: A Biographical and Autobiographical Study of 100 Silent Film Actors and Actresses*. University Press of Kentucky.

Slide, Anthony (2004) *Silent Topics: Essays of Undocumented Areas of Silent Film*, Scarecrow Press.

Spears, Jack (1977) *The Civil War on the Screen*, A.S. Barnes

Stenn, David (1988) *Clara Bow, Runnin' Wild*, Cooper Square Press

Tibbetts, John, James M. Welsh (2010) *American Classic Screen Interviews*, Scarecrow Press

Warren, Patricia (1989) *Elstree: The British Hollywood*, Virgin Books

Archives / Collections Consulted

The Academy of Motion Picture Arts and Sciences, Margaret Herrick Library, Los Angeles

- The Adolph Zukor Collection

- Paramount Pictures, Production Files

- James Wong Howe Collection

- The Hollywood Museum Collection

George Eastman House Museum, Rochester, New York

New York Public Library

The Library of Congress, Washington

British Film Institute

National Archive, Britain

Photoplay Productions

University College Dublin

Irish Film Institute

American Film Institute

Herbert Brenon

Dublin City

Charles Stewart Parnell

Kingstown, County Dublin, birthplace of Herbert Brenon

Herbert Brenon in fighting form.

Minneapolis

Herbert Brenon directing *Ivanhoe.*

Carl Laemmle, Founder of Universal

California in the early days

Actress, Leslie Carter

A Daughter of the Gods

Annette Kellerman

The White House

Herbert Brenon and Alla Nazimova during the filming of
War Brides

Herbert Brenon directing a scene.

Herbert Brenon in 1915

New Jersey was among the most popular film locations in the early days

The Fall of the Romanoffs

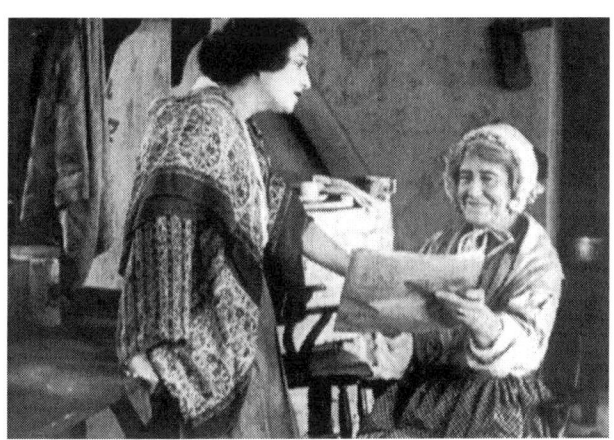

Dame Ellen Terry in *Invasion of Britain*

Marie Doro and Herbert Brenon in the Mediterranean

Herbert Brenon

The talented Norma Talmadge

New York

James Wong Howe and Herbert Brenon on location

New York Streetscape

Pola Negri

Jesse Lasky

Herbert Brenon on location

J.M. Barrie

Betty Bronson, Herbert Brenon and Mary Pickford

The Street of Forgotten Men

Clara Bow

Beau Geste

Alice Joyce and Mary Brian

Herbert Brenon loved to sail

Herbert Brenon, in his California days.

Illustrations Courtesy of :

Photoplay Productions,

Kevin Brownlow

George Eastman House Museum

Library of Congress, Washington

New York Public Library

Author's Collection

Newspapers and Periodicals consulted

American Film Institute Index of Feature Films, American
Cinematographer, Cornishman, Chester Chronicle, Chicago Tribune,
Cinematograph Exhibitors Mail, Daily Capital Journal, Daily Express,
Daily Illini, Daytona Beach Morning Journal, Evening Ledger, El Paso
Herald, Film Daily, Gotham Weekly Gazette, The Guardian, Griffithania,
Hartford Courant, Irish Times, Irish Independent, The Implet, Kine
Weekly, Los Angeles Times, Monroe City Democrat, Moving Picture
World, Motion Picture News, Motion Picture Classic, New York Times,
New York Dramatic Mirror, New York Globe, New York Morning
Telegraph, New York Clipper, Observer, Picturegoer, Picture Play,
Photoplay,The Plattsburgh Sentinel, Pullman Herald, Quincy Daily
Journal, Seattle Star, Sunday Independent, San Francisco Bulletin, Sydney
Morning Herald, The Times, Time magazine, Universal Weekly, Variety,
Washington Herald, The Washington Post, The Washington Times, Wid's
Weekly, Winona Republican Herald, Yale University Daily News.

About the Author

Ian Graham is a filmmaker and film historian with expertise in the field of American Cinema. He holds an MA Degree in Film Studies, from University College Dublin, and has lectured in Film Studies.

iangrahamfilm@gmail.com

Printed in Great Britain
by Amazon